Acquisition Appraisal

To

Kim

Ain't nothing like you in the shade of a tree
when you're off in a dream and your hair is a mess
I turn my eyes to the sky and I give thanks to the Lord
that he planted a tree and then handed me this.

Sko/Torp (1994): A Touch Of My Hand.

Helle Langhoff Lønroth

Acquisition Appraisal

Presenting and Testing the Financial Theories

DJØF Publishing Copenhagen
1996

Acquisition Appraisal
Presenting and Testing the Financial Theories
First Edition 1996

DJØF Publishing is a company of the
Association of Danish Lawyers and Economists

Printed in Denmark 1996
by Narayana Press, Gylling

ISBN 87-574-0431-3

DJØF Publishing
133 Gothersgade
P.O.B. 126
DK-1015 Copenhagen K
Denmark

Phone: +45 33 95 97 00
Fax: +45 33 95 99 97
E-mail: fl@djoef.dk
Homepage: http://www.djoef/flhome.htm

Contents

Foreword

During the last 10 years, both in Denmark and abroad, the number of company acquisitions has increased and has resulted in extensive changes in established branch structures and competitive conditions. These acquisitions have also affected the daily routines and opportunities of many employees. Historically, the tendency has been for company acquisitions and mergers to occur in waves; but now the tendency seems to be, to a large extent, for acquisitions and mergers to occur across country borders. The problem with this is that acquisitions involving foreign companies often entail greater uncertainty and risk than otherwise, affecting the probability that a company's expected profits can actually be realized.

Many dissertations and investigations have been carried out within the field, especially ones looking into the motives and causes behind acquisitions and mergers. However, not many of these dissertations and investigations have focused on the consequences or results of company acquisitions and mergers nor have they asked: If acquisitions are a good investment? Who benefits from a company acquisition? Are the gains from acquisitions overestimated? Is the probability for better results higher if an acquiring company does its homework prior to acquisition?

The author of the work presented here has posed and answered these central and other related questions. Her purpose has been two-sided: to analyse how the stock market financially appraises a long series of foreign acquisitions carried out by Danish concerns in the period 1988-1992 and to identify acquisition motives and practices from the acquiring companies' point of view.

The work also provides a skilful insight into how a population of Danish companies work in practice with acquisitions: the methods they use to assign value to acquired foreign entities; and the experience they have accumulated in the course of negotiations, during the following integration phase, etc. With this background, it is hoped that this publication will inspire practitioners and consultants to master the complicated acquisition process. This work will also serve as useful guidance for the theoretically interested.

The author of this work, Helle Langhoff Lønroth, Ph.D., is an assistant professor with the Department of International Business at the Aarhus School of Business. For several years, her research has focused on companies' acquisitions from a financial point of view.

Professor Jesper Strandskov, dr. merc.
Department of International Business
Aarhus School of Business, August 1996

CHAPTER 1

Introduction

1. Topic of the Book

Over the last two decades, and especially since the mid-1980's, the amount of Danish foreign direct investment (FDI) has increased. During the period 1986-1990, this number increased by 41%, reaching 859 in 1990.[1] Furthermore, the proportion of FDI carried out as acquisitions also increased. Acquisitions accounted for 29% of Danish FDI after 1986, as opposed to 15% before 1984.[2]

Despite the increasing importance of acquisitions as a form of Danish FDI, this topic has received only limited attention among Danish scholars. This is perhaps not surprising given the lack of current, public statistics on the subject.[3]

In their study of Danish FDI, Pedersen et al. (1993) give only a few characteristics of Danish foreign acquisitions. First and foremost, acquired companies were, on average, larger than those companies begun as green-field investments. Second, most companies (91%) were acquired solely by Danish companies, i.e., wholly-owned acquisitions, rather than by partnerships, e.g., with the previous owner or with other investors. Third, the average number of employees was larger when the acquisitions were made jointly with the previous owner (331) than when the acquisitions were 100% Danish (99).[4] Most of the Danish companies in the study by Pedersen et al. (1993) mentioned »access to the foreign market« as the primary motive for their FDI, i.e., both green-field investments and acquisitions.

1 Schultz et al. (1986), Table 3.8, and Pedersen et al. (1993) Table 1.

2 Pedersen et al. (1993), Table 16.

3 KonkurrenceRådet (The Competition Council) publishes statistics on mergers and acquisitions in Denmark every year, but they do not keep a record of Danish foreign acquisitions. In 1992, however, KonkurrenceRådet quite exceptionally collected data on Danish foreign acquisitions using information published in newspapers and journals. This data is published in KonkurrenceRådet (1993). Furthermore, since 1988, the Danish National Bank has kept, as a part of their currency statistics, statistics on FDI in DKK, divided by type of investment, including acquisitions. These statistics are available from the Danish National Bank upon request.

4 Pedersen et al. (1993), Table 15.

not react fairly or correctly when new information, e.g., annual reports or investment decisions, is announced to the market.[12] To some extent, we might compare the price-generating process with a black box. We see a piece of new information enter the black box and the price reaction pops out; thus, we assume a cause-effect link. But maybe there is more than one item of information or maybe that item is only one is a series of items. Or maybe market participants have already incorporated a part of the news in the price. Maybe they guessed what would happen. Maybe they guessed wrong. There are a lot of »maybe's« to confuse the picture of a clear cause-effect relationship. The same »maybe's« create methodological problems.[13]

Although scholars seek continuously to diminish methodological problems, it is necessary to examine both levels of analysis, i.e., the company and stock market perspectives, to give a fair answer to the question as to whether effects observed in the stock market are valid for the companies themselves.

Related to the performance issue is the question of how acquiring companies reach their decisions to acquire. First and foremost, an evaluation of performance must be seen in relation to the purpose at hand. This issue has been studied frequently in the area of strategy. Second, it is relevant to examine to what extent the »tools«, i.e., theories, models and rules of thumb, are applicable in acquisition appraisal, and subsequently whether these »tools« give a correct appraisal. To my knowledge, this has not been examined before.

The complex of problems presented above form the sphere of interest of this book. In the next section, the aim of the book will be presented.

2. Aim of the Book

There are two related aims of this book, namely:

1. *to account for the theories on the financial appraisal of acquisitions, and*
2. *to test these theories empirically, to the extent possible.*

In this context, financial appraisal includes both *the stock market's appraisal*, i.e., the stock price reaction to the announcement of an acquisition, and *the acquiring company's appraisal,* i.e., its appraisal of the company which subsequently is acquired. This means that the focus of this book is delimited to the investment appraisals leading to a positive result - in this incidence an acquisition. Furthermore, because the financial appraisal of acquisitions is seen from two perspectives, i.e., the stock market's and the acquiring company's, the two related aims of this book will be addressed from each of these perspectives. This is necessary because the two

---

[12] See, for example, Ugebrevet Mandag Morgen (1994), in which a number of Danish managers express their perception of whether the Danish stock market's reaction to new information is fair/correct.

[13] Chapter 3.1.1 deals with some of the problems in event study methodology.

perspectives are understood at different empirical levels of analysis and operate with different - although not colliding - theoretical foundations.

From each of the perspectives on financial appraisal of acquisitions, it holds that the theoretical foundations consist of a series of related theories - or what Lakatos refers to as »research programmes«.[14] Within a research programme, there are certain assumptions common to all of the theories belonging to the research programme. These assumptions are taken as given and are not questioned. In addition to these, there are other assumptions that differ among the theories in the research programme, and they, as well as the explanations rendered by the theories, may be questioned by other theories belonging to the research programme.

In this book, Lakatos' theory on research programmes, called the Methodology of Scientific Research Programmes (MSRP), will be used as an explanatory framework for addressing the first aim of this book, i.e., *to account for the theories on the financial appraisal of acquisitions.*

The following questions will be addressed with respect to each of the two views on acquisition appraisal:

- To which research programme does the theory belong?
- What are the premises of the theory?
- Which predictions can logically be deduced from the theory's premises?

Addressing these questions will also reveal the current state of the art for each of the perspectives on financial acquisition appraisal. Moreover, by clarifying the premises and assertions resulting from the theories, these questions will also clarify to what extent it is possible to test the theories empirically, i.e., the questions form a bridge to the second aim of this book, which is: *to test these theories empirically to the extent possible.* The purpose of the second aim is to examine the empirical support for these theories to the extent this is possible.

A sample of Danish foreign acquisitions made during the period January 1, 1988 December 31, 1992 will be used in this investigation. The choice to use data on Danish company acquisition is partly motivated by my background[15] and partly motivated by the shortfall of empirical examinations of Danish foreign acquisitions.[16] So the opportunity is present for using »fresh« data to test the theories.

In working with the second aim, it is emphasized that the theories will only be tested *to the extent this is possible.* This is due to limitations in the possibilities for

---

[14] Lakatos (1970) defines a »research programme« as a successive number of theories having a certain familiarity, i.e., a common hard core, and negative and positive heuristics. In Chapter 1.3.2, Lakatos' theory on research programmes, the methodology of scientific research programmes, is further elaborated.

[15] I am *Danish*, and I was granted a PhD scholarship in mid-September *1992* at the Department of *International Business*, the Aarhus School of Business.

[16] Similarly, there are no current, public statistics on Danish foreign acquisitions.

testing theories and thus checking their empirical validity.[17] There are several reasons why the possibility for testing a theory may be limited.

First, not all theories can be empirically tested. Logical theories are an example of such theories. Logical theories can be defined as theories based on rational reasoning, without empirical postulates about the human behavior their use depends on.[18] Logic is the study of correct reasoning. In logical theories, logic is used to deduce conclusions from assertions; thus these theories are true by definition. Thus, as logical theories are true by definition, it is not possible to falsify these theories empirically. But it is possible, though, to test empirically whether the theory is working in a real-life situation, i.e., the theory's operationality and the validity of its statements, as expressed by H. Nørreklit (1991):[19]

» *In order to work,*

- *a model or a theory must be operational and*
- *the statements of the model or theory must be valid*

By operationality, I understand that the theory or model can be applied concretely. By validity, I understand that the reality reacts either according to the purpose or as prescribed in the model.«

Second, the extent to which empirical theories, i.e., theories that make empirical postulates about actual relationships in the definite and directly observable reality, can be tested depends on the methods as well as the data currently available.

Although a theory is not or is only partly testable at a certain point in time, methods can be developed in the future enabling a more thorough or severe test of the theory. Similarly, a theory which has been falsified using simple, but currently available methods might be restored when more sophisticated methods are employed. Thus, when testing theories, it is also necessary to focus on the methods used for testing the theories and to specify their assumptions - direct as well as implicit assumption.

The availability of data can also restrict the possible tests a theory can be subjected to. Access and cost may limit the data available for testing and thus weaken the test. It is, therefore, necessary to consider the possible restraints place on the tests by the data.

The limitations on empirically testing the theories will likely vary with the perspective taken on financial acquisition appraisal due to the difference in theoretical foundation. Because of this, the specific research questions posed while exploring the second aim will also vary with these perspectives. Thus, with respect

---

17 As will be made apparent from the methodological considerations in Chapter 1.3.3, some emphasis is placed on criticism and the empirical testing of theories.

18 This definition is adapted from H. Nørreklit (1993).

19 p. 135; author's translation.

to the research questions addressing the second aim, these can preliminarily[20] be formulated under the following two headings:

Research questions related to the stock market's appraisal:
Is it possible to test the Danish stock market's appraisal of Danish foreign acquisitions, and if so, how the stock market appraised the acquisitions? Can the differences in the stock market's appraisal of different types of acquisitions - which different theories prescribe - also be found in the Danish sample? Or is it possible to falsify some of these theories by dismissing either the theories' predictions or their assumptions?

Research questions related to the acquiring company's appraisal:
Is it possible to test the acquiring company's appraisal, and if so, how they actually appraised the companies they acquired? Which theories are applied in the appraisal? What restrictions inhibit the operationability of these theories in reality? How can the operationalization of these theories be improved?

3. Methodological Considerations

The purpose of this section is to present the basic meta-theoretical assumptions of this book, i.e., the guidelines that have determined the research presented in this book.

Because my understanding of the scientific ideal is very much influenced by the work of Karl R. Popper, critical rationalism has been chosen as the methodological basis for this study. Furthermore, the scientific ideal in the area of finance is clearly a rational one - and perhaps even to a certain extent a critically rational one. So the methods used in finance will still be applicable for this study, even if the empiricism has a different importance in *critical* rationalism. Chapter 1.3.1 presents the essence of Popper's scientific ideal, i.e., his schema of the scientific process is along with its implications for different categories of theories.

Critical rationalism is a normative theory of science, and as such, it represents the scientific ideal used in this book. However, we know that reality does not always correspond to our ideals. Thus, in Chapter 1.3.2, I have chosen to present a descriptive theory of science, as represented by the work of Imre Lakatos, yet another critical rationalist. In his MSRP, Imre Lakatos proposes how science actually evolves. MSRP willl be used later in this study as a framework for explaining the development of financial theories on acquisition appraisal.

Chapter 1.3.3 argues for the relevance of the chosen methodology and briefly presents the methods applied in this study. The methods will be elaborated on in depth in the chapters where they are applied.

---

20 The research questions will be elaborated further in Chapters 3.2.1 and 3.3.1, with respect to the appraisal by the stock market, and in Chapter 5.1, with respect to the appraisal by the acquiring company.

3.1. Critical Rationalism (Karl R. Popper)

The most well-known contribution of Popper is probably his criterion of demarcation between science and pseudo-science. In this Popper basically propose that in order to be scientific a theory has to be refutable i.e., empirically testable. Inevitably Popper's criterion of demarcation has caused quite some stir within the area of social science since far from all theories in this area are testable. However in their focus on »testability« Popper's critiques often overlook what in my view is the significant contribution of Popper's criterion of demarcation is the focus on what might be called »critical attitude« in science. By proposing bold theories and by criticizing and trying to refute our theories - even those we like the most - we hope to uncover their weak spots. When we face a number of weak spots in a theory, the rational procedure, according to Popper, would then be to develop - by conjectures and refutations - a new and better theory, i.e,. a theory that includes the old theory's forces and at the same time overcomes its weak spots. In other words, criticism - or critical method - is a method for seeking out new problems.[21] Problems may lead to the development of new and improved theories to which the critical method is also applied, refuted and replaced by even better theories. Thus, the critical method is, in fact, the method by which we try to make scientific growth. Popper's view of the scientific process can thus be summarized as follows:[22]

$$P_1 \rightarrow T_1 \rightarrow D_1 \rightarrow E_1 \rightarrow P_2 \rightarrow T_2 \rightarrow D_2 \rightarrow E_2 \rightarrow P_3 \rightarrow \ldots$$

---

21 Compare this with the first italics in the quotation in the next footnote.

22 This schematic view of the scientific process is adopted from Magee (1973), p.51. It differs from Popper in the respect that it has an extra term, D. See Popper (1972), p. 287, author's italics: »I shall, therefore, before going any further into my topic, present a general tetradic schema which I have found more and more useful as a description of the growth of theories. It is as follows:

$$P_1 \rightarrow TT \rightarrow EE \rightarrow P_2.$$

Here P stands for »problem«; TT stands for »tentative theory«; and EE stands for »(attempted) error-elimination«, especially by way of critical discussion. My tetradic schema is an attempt to show that *the result of criticism, or of error-elimination, applied to a tentative theory, is as a rule the emergence of a new problem*; or, indeed, of several new problems. Problems, after they have been solved and their solutions properly examined, tend to beget problem-children: new problems, often of greater depth and ever greater fertility than the old ones. This can be seen especially in the physical sciences; and I suggest that we can best gauge the progress made in any science by the distance in depth and expectedness between P1 and P2: the best tentative theories (*and all theories are tentative*) are those which give rise to the deepest and most unexpected problems.«

where:

P_1: a problem
T_1: a bold conjecture about the solution of the problem; i.e., a tentative theory[23]
D_1: assertions deduced from the theory
E_1: error-elimination; i.e., attempt to refute the theory using empirical tests and critical method
P_2: a new problem
T_2: a new theory - chosen by competing theories - to replace the old theory
D_2: assertions deduced from the theory
E_2: error-elimination; i.e., attempt to refute the theory using empirical tests and critical method
P_3: a new problem

In relation to the scientific process as described above, it is necessary for the sake of clarity to elaborate a bit further on its different parts and especially on »problems«, »error-elimination« and when a refuted theory can be replaced by a new theory.

First, even if the term »problem« is very central to Popper's ideas, he makes no attempt to define it, although there are several vague or implicit definitions of »problems« or »problem situations«, as is evident in the following three quotations: [24] [25] [26]

»For a problem is a difficulty, and understanding a problem consists in finding out that there is a difficulty, and where the difficulty lies.«

»Problems crop up especially when we are disappointed in our expectations, or when our theories involve us in difficulties, in contradictions; and they may arise either within a theory, or between two different theories, or as the result of a clash between our theories and our observations.«

»»Try to learn what people are discussing nowadays in science. Find out where the difficulties arise, and take an interest in disagreements. These are the questions which you should take up.« In other words, you should study the *problem situation* of the day.«[27]

---

[23] In the rest of this scheme, »theory« is equal to »tentative theory«. Note the second phrase in italics in the quotation in the previous footnote.

[24] Popper (1972), p. 181.

[25] Popper (1963), p. 222.

[26] Popper (1963), p. 129.

[27] The quotation is taken from the following context: »All this means that a young scientist who hopes to make discoveries is badly advised if this teacher tells him, »Go round and observe«, and that he is well advised if his teacher tells him:« . . . »This means that you pick up, and try to continue, a line of inquiry which has the whole background of the earlier development of science behind it; you fall in with the tradition or science. It is a very simple and decisive point, but nevertheless one that is often not sufficiently realized by rationalists - that we cannot start afresh; that we must make use of what people before us have done in science.« Popper (1963), p. 129.

From the quotations above, it is evident that Popper first and foremost is interested in the problems of the day, i.e,. not »the initial problem«, P_1, but rather the problems which »crop up« as a result of error-elimination somewhere in the scientific process. In this way, problems are important in that they challenge us to make better theories and hereby contribute to the growth of scientific knowledge.

When a new problem arises, the next step - according to Popper's schema - is to propose a bold conjecture about the solution to the problem. Popper does not believe there exists any logical method for coming up with a new theory; the best we can do is simply guess! After proposing a theory, the assertions that can be deduced from the theory should be clarified so error-elimination can begin.

Second, in error-elimination, scientific theories are both criticized and tested empirically. Criticizism unveils the vulnerable points of the theory, and to Popper, it is preferable if the criticism is imaginative. As he says:[28]

». . . *imaginative criticism* . . . is how we transcend our local and temporal environment by trying to think of circumstances *beyond* our experience: by criticizing the universality, or the structural necessity, of what may, to us appear (or what philosophers may describe) as the »given« or as »habit«; by trying to find construct, invent, new situations - that is, *test* situations, *critical* situations; and by trying to locate, detect, and challenge our prejudices and habitual assumptions.«

With respect to scientific theories, criticism precedes empirical testing in the error-elimination process during which the vulnerable points of the theory are confronted with observations in the attempt to refute it.

But what about non-scientific theories? Even if they are irrefutable by definition,[29] we still need to distinguish between true and false (or good and bad) theories.

---

[28] Popper (1972), p.148.

[29] That a non-empirical theory per definition will be true if it is consistent is evident from the following figure; Popper (1989) p.19:

	IDEAS *that is*	
DESIGNATIONS or TERMS or CONCEPTS		STATEMENTS or PROPOSITIONS or THEORIES
	may be formulated in	
WORDS		ASSERTIONS
	which may be	
MEANINGFUL		TRUE
	and their	
MEANING		TRUTH
	may be reduced, by way of	
DEFINITIONS		DERIVATIONS
	to that of	
UNDEFINED CONCEPTS		PRIMITIVE PROPOSITIONS
	the attempt to establish (rather than reduce) by these means their	
MEANING		TRUTH
	leads to an infinite regress	

According to Popper, criticism is still the main instrument for accomplishing this. Popper distinguishes between two types of non-scientific theories:

1. logical and mathematical theories
2. philosophical and meta-physical theories[30]

Popper explains the difference between empirical theories and logical /mathematical theories in the following manner:[31]

»In so far as a calculus is applied to reality, it loses the character of a *logical* calculus and becomes a descriptive theory *which may be empirically refutable*; and in so far as it is treated as irrefutable, i.e. as a system of *logically true* formulae, rather than a descriptive scientific theory, it is not applied to reality.«

The procedure of distinguishing between true and false logical and mathematical theories is fundamentally the same as that for empirical and scientific theories, except for the lack of empirical arguments: In Popper's words: [32]

»Whenever we find a mathematical theory of which we do not know whether is true or false we test it, first superficially and then more severely, by trying to refute it. If we are unsuccessful we then try to prove it or to refute its negation. If we fail again, doubts as to the truth of the theory may have cropped up again, and we shall again try to refute it, and so on, until we either reach a decision or else shelve the problem as too difficult for us.«

So even if logical and mathematical theories are empirically irrefutable, it is possible to refute them within the framework of formal logic or mathematics. The distinction between true and false theories is a bit more blurred when it comes to philosophical or metaphysical theories. It is not possible to test meta-physical or philosophical theories empirically nor though the use of a formal system of logic or mathematics. But it is possible to discuss both meta-physical and philosophical theories critically in the context of their problem-situation. Popper states: [33]

»Now if we look upon a theory as a proposed solution to a set of problems, then the theory immediately lends itself to critical discussion - even if it is non-empirical and irrefutable. For we can now ask questions such as, Does it solve the problem? Does it solve it better than other theories? Has it perhaps merely shifted the problem? Is the solution simple? Is it fruitful? Does it perhaps contradict other philosophical theories needed for solving other problems? Questions of this kind show that a critical discussion even of irrefutable theories may well be possible.«

---

[30] For example, determinism, idealism and irrationalism, but also critical rationalism. For further elaboration of Popper's understanding of a philosophical theory, see Popper (1963), p. 193+.

[31] Popper (1963), p. 210.

[32] Popper (1963), p. 197.

[33] Popper (1963), p. 199.

Thus the use of critical discussion enables us to reach a conclusion as to whether a specific meta-physical or philosophical theory, in our opinion, is true or false or whether we merely prefer one theory over another. In this way, criticism can be applied to all theories including non-scientific ones.

The two elements in error-elimination of a scientific theory, criticism and tests, are included in what Popper calls a theory's corroboration (or degree of corroboration):[34]

»By the degree of corroboration of a theory I mean a concise report evaluating the state (at a certain time *t*) of the critical discussion of a theory, with respect to the way it solves its problems; its degree of testability; the severity of tests it has undergone; and the way it has stood up to these tests. Corroboration (or degree of corroboration) is thus an evaluating *report of past performance. . . . But it says nothing whatever about future performance, or about the »reliability« of a theory.*«

In the schema of the scientific process, corroboration can be used to choose among competing theories at a certain point in time. This lead us to the elaboration of the final part of the schema, namely, when a refuted theory can be replaced by a new theory. Also in this respect, Popper is more interested in giving guidelines to how progress is ensured in science rather than explaining how science actually develops. According to Popper, it is possible to know whether a certain scientific theory is better - in terms of scientific progress - than another scientific theory, even before any of them have been tested empirically. Popper calls this the criterion of relative potential satisfactoriness or potential progressiveness:[35]

»It [the criterion of relative potential satisfactoriness; author's note] characterizes as preferable the theory which tells us more; that is to say, the theory which contains the greater amount of empirical information or *content*; which is logically stronger; which has the greater explanatory and predictive power; and which can therefore be *more severely tested* by comparing predicted facts with observations. In short, we prefer an interesting, daring, and highly informative theory to a trivial one.«

A new theory which possesses more content than the old theory is one that explains not only the successful predictions of its predecessor, but also some (or all) of the refuted predictions of its predecessor. This requirement, allowing for a more severe test of the new theory, serves the purpose of protecting the old - and perhaps even refuted - theory against new theories which do not represent genuine scientific progress.

---

[34] Popper (1972), p. 18.

[35] Popper (1963), p. 217.

In addition to this, Popper also requires that the new theory be independently testable. This excludes the use of *ad hoc* definitions or *ad hoc* theories.[36]

All this sums up to Popper's three requirements for the growth of knowledge:[37]

»1. the new theory should proceed from some *simple, new and powerful, unifying idea* about some connection or relationship between hitherto unconnected things or facts or new »theoretical entities«;
2. the new theory should be *independently testable*; and
3. the theory should pass some new, and severe, tests, i.e.,
   a) it should be successful in some of its new predictions and
   b) it should not be refuted too soon - that is, before it has been strikingly successful.«

The purpose of these criteria and rules and critical method is to secure that scientific theories are not made »immune« to refutation, and also to secure that a falsified scientific theory is only replaced when the new theory represents genuine scientific progress. The criterion of relative potential satisfactoriness helps us to choose among competing theories *before* these have been tested. But even if a new theory fulfils the criterion of relative potential satisfactoriness, it is not sufficient to replace the old and falsified theory immediately. Because we wish to insure genuine scientific progress, a new theory which *can* be more severely tested *should* be tested in this way. So if, and only if, the new theory is better corroborated than the old, falsified theory, then the new theory replaces the old and falsified theory. Thus, the corroboration of theories helps us to choose among competing theories *after* they have been tested and, as critical rationalists, we prefer the theory which has the highest corroboration, i.e., the one which appears to be the best so far.

3.2. The Methodology of Scientific Research Programmes (MSRP) (Imre Lakatos)

Although Lakatos puts great emphasis on Popper's theories,[38] he does not find that they describe the history of science accurately. For example, Lakatos claims - contrary to Popper, but more in line with Kuhn's paradigm concept - that:[39]

»...the typical descriptive unit of great scientific achievements is not an isolated hypothesis but rather a research programme.«

To explain how science has evolved historically, Lakatos proposes the theory of *the methodology of scientific research programmes* (MSRP), and in this he uses

---

[36] Cf. Popper (1972), pp. 15-16: »*Ad hoc* explanations are explanations which are not independently testable, that is, of the effect to be explained.«

[37] Popper (1963), pp. 241-247.

[38] See, for example, Lakatos (1978), p. 139.

[39] Lakatos (1978), p. 4. A research programme is a series of theories that are connected by a common »hard core«. Compare with descriptions later in the text.

»research programme« as the descriptive unit. A research programme is a series of theories that are connected by a common »hard core« - a theory or a set of assumptions,[40] and a set of methodological rules - the research programme's negative and positive heuristics. Lakatos characterizes scientific research programmes[41] in the following manner:[42]

»All scientific research programmes may be characterized by their »*hard core*«. The negative heuristic of the programme forbids us to direct the *modus tollens* at this »hard core«. Instead, we must use our ingenuity to articulate or even invent »auxiliary hypotheses« which form a *protective belt* around this core, and we must redirect the *modus tollens* to *these*. It is this protective belt of auxiliary hypotheses which has to bear the brunt of tests and get adjusted and re-adjusted, or even completely replaced, to defend the thus-hardened core. A research programme is successful if all this leads to a progressive problemshift; unsuccessful if it leads to a degenerating problemshift. «

Thus, the negative heuristic tells us not to hastily accept falsification of the hard core despite a divergence between observations and the assertions deduced from the research programme. Instead we should focus on the hints and suggestions given by the positive heuristic of the research programme as to how to develop auxiliary hypothesis explaining the discovered divergence. If this procedure succeeds, one or more of the theories in the protective belt will be adjusted or even replaced, i.e., refuted, in order to explain the divergence and protect the hard core of the research programme. In this respect the MSRP's criterion for the refutation of a theory is rather similar to that of Popper's: According to Lakatos (1978):[43]

»*Within* a research programme a theory can only be eliminated by a better theory, that is, by one which has excess empirical content over its predecessors, some of which is subsequently confirmed.«[44]

The success - or progress - of a research programme can be assessed on a »stand alone« basis as well as in comparison with competing research programmes. As explained by Lakatos (1978):[45]

---

40 The hard core can be a theory, even a meta-physical theory (Lakatos (1970), p. 12 note) as well as a set of assumptions (Lakatos (1970), p. 133.)

41 Note: Lakatos claims that only research programmes, and not single theories, should be classified as »scientific« or »meta-physical«.

42 Lakatos (1970), p. 133. Note: »*Modus tollens*: a logical deduction formula where one deduces from a universal theory to a singularly observation statement and on the basis hereof decides whether the universal theory is falsified or not.« Knudsen (1991), p. 342; author's translation.

43 p. 112.

44 See also:»...according to the methodology of scientific research programmes, no accepted basic statement *alone* entitles the scientist to reject a theory.« Lakatos (1978), p. 111.

45 p. 112 and note.

»A research programme is said to be *progressing* as long as its theoretical growth anticipates its empirical growth, that is, as long as it keeps predicting novel facts with some success (»*progressive problemshift*«); it is *stagnating* if its theoretical growth lags behind its empirical growth, that is, as long as it gives only *post hoc* explanations either of chance discoveries or of facts anticipated by, and discovered in, a rival programme (»*degenerating problemshift*«). In fact, I define a research programme as degenerating even if it anticipates novel facts but does so in a patched-up development rather than by a coherent, pre-planned positive heuristic. I distinguish three types of *ad hoc* auxiliary hypothesis: those which have no excess empirical content over their predecessor (»*ad* hoc_1«), those which do have such excess content but none of it is corroborated (»*ad* hoc_2«) and finally those which are not *ad hoc* in these two senses but do not form an integral part of the positive heuristics (»*ad* hoc_3«).«

In the description of a progressive research programme above, the influence of Popper is again evident[46] as it is in Lakatos' view on *the ad hoc* hypothesis. When a research programme is assessed on a stand alone basis, e.g., in the absence of a rival, it is of course possible to determine whether it is successful or not. But if the latter is the case, i.e., if the research programme is degenerating, the MSRP does not classify the research programme as refuted or rejected. In the MSRP framework, a research programme is only rejected when the work on it ceases .[47] This is evidently most likely when there are two competing research programmes - one progressive and the other degenerating.[48] Still, according to Lakatos, a degenerating research programme may very well become progressive again, and this is why a quick rejection is not necessarily positive. The same may be true for new, emerging research programmes, which leads Lakatos to conclude:[49]

»As opposed to Popper the methodology of scientific research programmes does not offer instant rationality. One must treat budding programmes leniently: programmes may take decades before they get off the ground and become empirically progressive.«

To summarize, in Lakatos' MSRP, research programmes are described by their hard core and their negative and positive heuristics. Furthermore, the MSRP classification of a research programme, as being progressing or stagnating or degenerating, is used both in the assessment of the research programme's evolution as well as in the comparison with competing research programmes.

46 Compare to Popper's criterion of relative potential satisfactoriness.

47 See Lakatos (1970), p.157fn.

48 »If a research programme progressively explains more than a rival, it »supersedes« it, and the rival can be eliminated (or, if you wish, »shelved«).« Lakatos (1978), p.112.

49 Lakatos (1978), p.6.

3.3. Choice and Criticism of Methodology

Critical rationalism has been chosen as the methodological basis for this study mainly because this book's conceptions of reality and of scientific ideal are congenial with that of Popper's. In the following, the methodological choice will be motivated further as well as criticized.

First and foremost, I agree with Popper's emphasis on criticism and empirical tests with respect to applied science, of which finance is an example. In applied science, error-elimination - or falsification - is to be seen as an excellent opportunity to learn from previous mistakes, and falsification thus becomes an important landmark: it signals the starting point for new scientific growth . Yet it has to be taken into account that falsification is less conclusive in the social sciences than it is in the natural sciences, as it is seldom possible to perform *crucial* experiments and tests. Moreover, falsification not only depends on the data available and the interpretation of facts, but it also depends on the quality and sophistication of the methods available for the testing. As a large proportion of these methods is based on mathematical and logical theories, the growth of these theories is also of great importance to the growth of those theories Popper labels »scientific«. Thus, even though I emphasize criticism and empirical tests, I still find Popper's criterion of demarcation between science and non-science to be to harsh.

Given the modifications elaborated above, critical rationalism serves as a relevant methodology for this book. In financial theory, which constitutes the theoretical core of this book, the prevailing methodology is clearly a rational one. But financial theories of acquisition appraisal have problems in explaining or being o-perationalized in reality, to a certain extent. Criticism and more focus on »real-life« within financial theories could be a fruitful approach for the theoretical growth in this area. As a method, criticism help us to identify the shortcomings of our theories and thus becomes a stepping-stone for scientific growth. Furthermore, when dealing with financial theories, it is vital to understand the distinction between logical and empirical theories. Logical theories, which have been the dominant research focus in the area of finance, cannot be operationalized in reality unless they are supplemented with an empirical basis transforming them into empirical and refutable theories.[50] To a certain extent, the empirical basis has been neglected, i.e., it has only received limited theoretical attention and consequently only limited testing. I believe this to be the reason for the limited use of some of the theories which the profession most recognizes. Developing the empirical basis that supplements logical theories in empirical theories, via the use of conjectures and refutations, is necessary for improving those theories, which are to be operationalized in reality. At the same time, this will almost surely increase the practitioner's use of our models, an important aim for many in this area.

Within the methodological framework outlined above, a number of methods are employed to achieve the aim of the book. The methods used either to test theories or to procure the data in this book, e.g., event studies, surveys or case study-

---

[50] See the distinction between logical and empirical theories in Chapter 1.3.1.

interviews, will not be accounted for here. They are covered in Parts 1 and 2. To obtain the greatest coherence within each of the two parts,[51] I have chosen to account for the employed methods in the context of relevant theories and data, i.e., where it relates in the book. In addition to these methods, Lakatos' MSRP is used in both parts. The MSRP is employed to account for and to evaluate the development in the state of the art in this research area. The MSRP is a relevant method for accomplishing this, being a descriptive theory on the history of science with a basis in the critical rationalist tradition.

4. Organization of the Book

This book presents two perspectives on the financial appraisal of acquisitions: the stock market's and the acquiring company's. The aims of this books - *to account for the theories on the financial appraisal of acquisitions* and *to test these theories empirically to the extent this is possible* - will be addressed for each of these perspectives in Parts 1 and 2, respectively.

Part 1 deals with acquisition appraisal from a stock market perspective and consists of Chapters 2 and 3. The first aim is addressed in Chapter 2, in which the theoretical foundation of the stock market perspective on the appraisal of acquisitions will be elaborated using Lakatos' MSRP as an explanatory framework. The second aim is addressed in Chapter 3, in which, first, the test method applied and the specific research question addressed are elaborated and, then, the results and the theoretical implications of the test are presented.

Part 2 deals with acquisition appraisal from an acquiring company perspective and consists of Chapters 4, 5 and 6. In Chapter 4, the first aim is addressed from the acquiring company's perspective on the appraisal of acquisitions and is addressed once again using Lakatos' MSRP as an explanatory framework. The theoretical foundation of this part of the book is not empirically testable. Thus, the second aim is addressed in a more indirect manner in Chapter 5, in which an examination is made of the operationability of the theories and related problems. The examination of the operationability of the theories also serves the purpose of identifying problem areas that a new and extended theory, applicable to acquisition appraisal from an acquiring company's perspective, should be able to cope with. Such a theory is presented in Chapter 6, in which the theoretical foundation of this part of the book is combined with an existing empirical theory and extended with a set of additional conjectures on acquisition appraisal.

In Chapter 7, the final chapter of the book, the main results as well as their theoretical and practical implications will be presented.

This constitutes the overall outline of the study. At the beginning of Parts 1 and 2, the aim of that part is elaborated in further detail. Similarly, at the beginning of each chapter, a more detailed outline of the chapter is given.

---

[51] See Chapter 1.4.

An overview of the two parts and their interrelations, as well as the level of analysis, is given in Figure 1.2.

Figure 1.2: Organization of the book

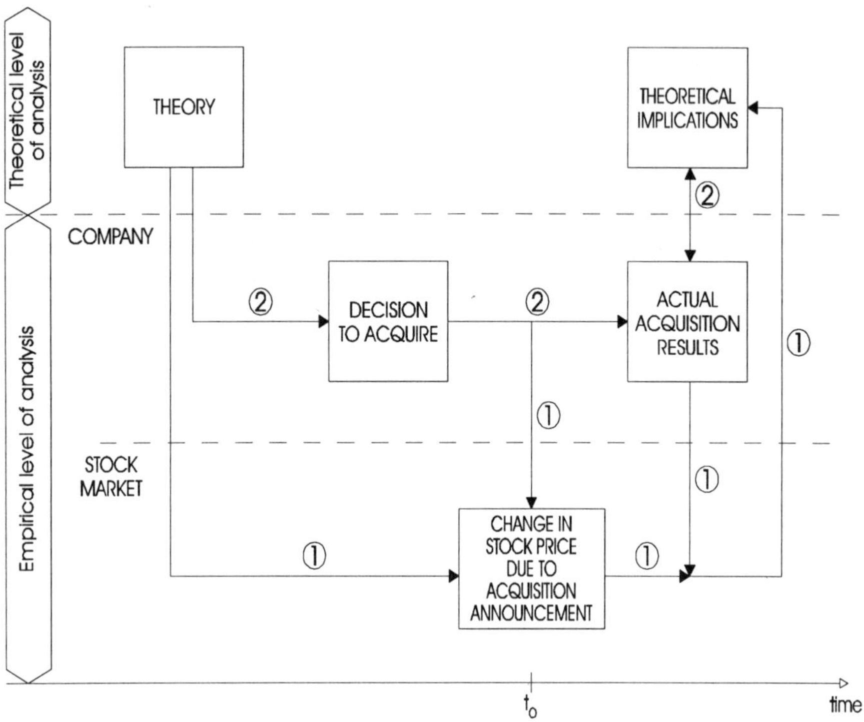

①: Relationship elaborated in part 1

②: Relationship elaborated in part 2.

PART 1

Acquisition Appraisal - The Stock Market Perspective

A dominant research question in the literature on acquisitions has been whether acquisitions are good investments for shareholders, i.e., whether acquisitions create shareholder wealth.[52] In this connection, this part of the book will deal with the stockholders' appraisal of acquisitions.

The structure in this book follows Popper's schema of the scientific process:[53] First the theoretical foundation is presented using Lakatos' MSRP as an explanatory framework.[54] Then assertions are deduced from the theories, i.e., the test-hypotheses are developed. Finally, the theories are tested empirically.

The theoretical foundation of this part of the book is the market efficiency research programme, presented in Chapter 2. The hard core of this research programme is the market efficiency hypothesis, and as such it forms the basic, irrefutable assumptions of the theories in the protective belt. The theories explaining the stock market's appraisal of acquisitions are all located in the protective belt of the market efficiency research programme. There are only two fully developed theories on this subject within the area of finance, namely Jensen's »free cash flow hypothesis« and Roll's »hubris hypothesis«. These theories do not distinguish between domestic and international acquisitions, nor do most of the studies testing or otherwise examining the topic. However, there have been a number of exploratory studies examining the relationship between international acquisitions and shareholder wealth creation.

The assertions deduced originally in Jensen's »free cash flow hypothesis« and Roll's »hubris hypothesis« are, respectively, presented in Chapter 2 in connection with the theories. But in order to take the restrictions and the characteristics of the data into account in the testing, the exact hypotheses to be tested are developed in Chapter 3. The test method, the data and the results of the tests are all presented in

---

52 The value of a stock to an investor is composed of two elements: its price and the dividend payment. A change in the shareholder value thus implies either a price change or a change in the dividend payment. A change in the price is most common.

53 See footnote 22.

54 See Chapter 1.3.2.

Chapter 3. The test methodology, i.e., event study methodology, makes it possible to examine the stock market's price reaction to an acquisition announcement. The data is stock market data, i.e., returns of companies listed on the Danish stock exchange, the same companies' announcements of foreign acquisitions, and additional data collected via a questionnaire conducted in these companies.

In addition to the event study, a test is conducted to examine the validity of one of the assumption of the hard core of the market efficiency research programme. The test method applied, the additional data needed, and the results are also presented in Chapter 3.

CHAPTER 2

The Market Efficiency Research Programme

A very central theory in finance, perhaps the single most important one, is the efficient market hypothesis. The efficient market hypothesis is a theory, about which many financial theories have evolved, including those on acquisition appraisal from a stock market perspective. As such, it constitutes the hard core in the research programme, which is labelled, in this book, the market efficiency research programme.

The market efficiency hypothesis will be presented in the first section of this chapter along with the most commonly used methods for testing, as they are a very integral part of the market efficiency hypothesis. In the second section, the negative and positive heuristics of the market efficiency research programme will be presented. This section will also deal with some of the anomalies of the market efficiency research programme. The third section of this chapter will present theories in the protective belt, although the presentation will be limited to acquisition theories. The final section of this chapter will present an assessment of the market efficiency research programme.

1. The Hard Core: The Efficient Market Hypothesis

The concept of »market efficiency« is widely used in economics. But within finance, which focuses on capital markets, it has come to have a very specific meaning, namely that at time *t*:

security prices reflect all available information

It thus implies it is not possible to make economic profits[55] by trading a security on the basis of an available set of information. This last implication is also the same as

---

[55] Generally, economic profit is adjusted for risk and is net of all costs (mainly transaction costs).

assuming that the pricing mechanism is a »fair game«.[56] When new information is incorporated into the price, a price reaction will be observed.[57] The price reaction is considered to be the market's assessment of the information's importance to the price of the asset traded. Due to the fair game assumption, the price reaction - and thus also the market's assessment - will be *unbiased.*[58] In finance, the above definition of market efficiency is referred to as *the efficient market hypothesis,* and it constitutes the hard core of the market efficiency research programme.

In the definition of the market efficiency hypothesis above, it is not self-evident what »available« includes. Over the years though, three categories of the market efficiency hypothesis have evolved, each dealing with a different subset of information, assumed to be available to the market:

1. The *weak form* of the efficient market hypothesis. Only information contained in the past price history of the market is available and subsequently:
   security prices reflect all information contained in the market's past price history.
2. The *semi-strong form* of the efficient market hypothesis. All public information is available (including that contained in the past price history of the market), and thus:
   security prices reflect all publically-available information.
3. The *strong form* of the efficient market hypothesis. All types of information, public or private, is available, so that:
   security prices reflect all publically and privately-available information.

As is evident from the definitions above, the amount of information required increases as the form of the market efficiency hypothesis strengthens. Note that this also implies that the weaker forms are contained in the stronger forms, and subsequently, a market cannot be semi-strong efficient if it is not also weak form efficient.[59]

As trading on the basis of private (i.e., insider) information is illegal in most markets, the strong form of market efficiency is regarded as the logical completion of a possible set of hypotheses, for the most part. In the words of Jensen (1978):[60]

---

56 See Elton & Gruber (1991), p. 402: »»Fair game« is a very descriptive term. It says that there is no way to use »information« available at a point in time (t) to earn a return above normal.«

57 It is possible that prices do not react to the information, e.g., if it is not believed to have any effect, but this will be ignored for the moment.

58 The implicit unbiasedness assumption is important to many of the theories in the protective belt of the research programme, see Chapter 2.4, and for this reason, I have chosen to clarify its origin here.

59 Similarly, a market cannot be strong form efficient if it is not also semi-strong form efficient and thus also weak form efficient. In this way, the different forms of market efficiency can be visualized as the famous Russian »babushka« dolls, where one is contained in the other!

60 p. 97.

»The Semistrong Form of the Efficient Market Hypothesis, represents the accepted paradigm and is what is generally meant by unqualified references in the literature to the »Efficient Market Hypothesis«.«

With respect to the set of information assumed available in the semi-strong form, Jensen (1978) further notes:[61]

»Of course, the precise meaning of »publicly available« must be defined to give the hypothesis content. In specific tests that definition is usually made clear, but exactly where those boundaries are in a general sense is something that will profitably receive more attention in the future.«

Despite the fact this was written more than a decade ago, the subject has only received limited attention - if at all. Although semi-strong form tests have been performed using a large range of different types of information, it is still not clear what the general definition of publically-available information is. Perhaps this is a consequence of the preference for testing and tailoring methods rather than further development of empirical theories within finance.

Surely, a number of test procedures have become a very integral part of the market efficiency hypothesis (or perhaps the reverse). This fact becomes more evident when it is considered that the efficient market hypothesis cannot be tested in itself, but has to be tested jointly with an equilibrium-pricing model. This is also referred to as the joint hypothesis problem. The joint test of market efficiency and equilibrium-pricing model is only a problem when the joint hypothesis is rejected.[62] But the problem has been »solved« by keeping the market efficiency hypothesis and by replacing/ developing the equilibrium-pricing model;[63] i.e., by developing new methods for testing.

The efficient market hypothesis, including its three forms, constitutes the hard core of the market efficiency research programme presented in this book. The semi-strong form of the market efficiency hypothesis is considered to be the valid working hypothesis; so even if the strong form is included in the core of the research programme, it is not assumed to be valid. Furthermore, an implication of the efficient market hypothesis is that the stock market's expectations of future price behavior - which are contained in the current prices - are assumed to be unbiased. The unbiasedness assumption is also included in the hard core of the market efficiency research programme.

---

61 p. 97.

62 That is, is it the equilibrium-pricing model that has been rejected or is it the market efficiency hypothesis?

63 In this respect the negative heuristic of the research programme has succeeded, see Chapter 2.3.

1.1. Methods Used for Testing the Market Efficiency Hypothesis

Because a number of test procedures are an integral part of the market efficiency hypothesis and because the market efficiency hypothesis actually originates from some of these tests, I have chosen to briefly present the principles behind the test procedures in the following. This will be done in the context of the relevant form of market efficiency, which the procedures are used to test, even though they rightfully belong to the protective belt of the market efficiency research programme.

The methods used for testing the weak form of market efficiency examine whether it is possible to predict future returns and to earn above-normal[64] profits by doing so. As there are an infinite numbers of approaches for predicting future returns, it is necessary to use a *specific* approach, and the test is thus limited to examining whether that approach can predict future returns. Furthermore, if the specific approach can be used to predict future returns on a given set of data, it has to be tested again on a new set of data, i.e., over a different time period or on a different market, before it is possible to reject weak form efficiency. This replication is necessary because it is always possible - even on random numbers - to find a specific approach that works on a given set of data. If the approach can be replicated on new data, the market efficiency hypothesis is rejected.[65] Among the methods most commonly used to test the weak form of market efficiency are the random walk model, the martingale model, the submartingale model, models assuming linear relationships of price behavior[66] and the »filter rule« method. In the following, the random walk model and the filter rule method will be presented. The random walk model is presented because it has played a very important historical role for the market efficiency hypothesis, and the filter rule method is presented because it is now the prevailing method used to test the weak form of the market efficiency hypothesis.

The random walk model is very connected to the efficient market hypothesis. It was the discovery by Kendall, that stock prices seemed to follow a random walk, which formed the foundation for the efficient market hypothesis. As stated by Brealey & Myers (1988):[67]

»...Maurice Kendall, was a distinguished statistician and the subject was the behavior of stock and commodity prices. Kendall had been looking for regular price cycles but to his surprise he could not find them. Each series appeared to be »a »wandering« one, almost as if once a week the Demon of Chance drew a random number...and added it to the current price to determine the next week's price.« In other words, prices seemed to follow a *random walk*.«

---

64 That is, a profit adjusted for risk and net of all costs (mainly transaction costs).

65 Actually it is the weak form of the market efficiency hypothesis that is rejected. But because the weak form is embedded in the semi-strong form as well as the strong form, these are also implicitly rejected.

66 For example, the correlation between successive price changes or the log of price differences.

67 p. 282.

Trying to confirm the random walk model on a given set of data is one way of confirming the weak form of the market efficiency hypothesis. However, the random walk model has strict assumptions,[68] and therefore, evidence rejecting the random walk model is not enough to reject the weak form of the market efficiency hypothesis.

The filter rule method is another way of testing the weak form of the market efficiency hypothesis. It has become a very popular method for testing because it is able to test complex return patterns and at the same time is very simple to use. The principle of a filter rule test can be described by the following two steps. First a trading rule is constructed. The trading rule is often constructed in the following manner; as expressed by Lønroth & Reeb (1994):[69]

»Purchase the stock when it rises by X% from the previous low and hold it until it declines by Y% from the subsequent high. At this time, sell the stock and hold cash. Maintain the cash position until the price rises by X%.«[70]

Second, the trading rule is tested on a given set of data and its return is compared to the return of a cash deposit or, more commonly, to a buy-and-hold strategy.[71] If the trading rule gives a higher return than the two other strategies, then it is possible to reject the weak form of market efficiency *if and only if* the trading rule once more can generate a higher return when it is replicated on a new set of data.

The implications of the weak form of market efficiency is that it is not possible to earn an above-normal profit by analyzing historical price behavior.

The methods for testing the semi-strong form of market efficiency examine whether prices adjust quickly to new information, i.e., when information is made publically available. If prices adjust quickly to new information, then it will not be possible to earn above-normal profits trading on the basis of the new information. A market is generally considered to be semi-strong form efficient if new information is fully incorporated into the prices within a few days. Tests of semi-strong form efficiency are commonly labeled *event studies,* as they focus on how an event, i.e.,

---

68 The random walk model assumes that successive returns are independent and that the returns are identically distributed over time. These assumptions are not necessarily preconditions for the weak form of market efficiency hypothesis because successive returns may very well be correlated without the possibility for earning above-normal returns.

69 p. 16.

70 The trading rule can be constructed in a more or less complex manner than this example. For example, it could be constructed according to the principles of technical analysis, a theory which claims it is possible to predict future price behavior from past price behavior.

71 A buy-and-hold strategy implies buying the stocks that are being tested in the beginning of the test period and selling them at the end of the period. The return generated using the buy-and-hold strategy is equal to the relevant economic profit, adjusted for risk of the tested stocks.

new information, is incorporated into the price. Event study methodology is elaborated on in detail in Chapter 3; it will not be dealt with any further in this chapter.

The implications of the semi-strong form of market efficiency is that it is not possible to earn above-normal profits by analyzing publically-available information.

As mentioned earlier, it is the semi-strong form of the market efficiency hypothesis that serves as the accepted working hypothesis in this area of research, whereas the strong form is mainly considered to be the logical completion of a possible sėt of hypotheses. The type of information contained only in the strong form of market efficiency, and not in the weaker forms of market efficiency, is private information. It is, however, difficult to get hold of private information or yet alone to determine it. The strong form of the market efficiency hypothesis is, therefore, tested indirectly by examining if it is possible for a group of market participants, believed to have access to private information, to earn above-normal profits. For this purpose, the market participants are grouped into a hierarchy, specifying the order of access to private information. Managers would rank highest in the hierarchy, followed by board members, major stock holders, security analysts and portfolio managers. Most tests of the strong form market efficiency hypothesis focus on security analysts and examine whether it is possible to earn above-normal profits by trading according to the advice of security analysts, only a few days before the advice is made public.

The implications of the strong form of market efficiency is that it is not possible to earn above-normal profits by utilizing private or any other type of information.

2. The Negative and Positive Heuristics of the Market Efficiency Research Programme

The negative and positive heuristics of the market efficiency research programme are concerned with giving direction on how and how not to develop the research programme so that the hard core is protected. The hard core of the market efficiency programme can be reduced to two assumptions:[72]

1. *security prices reflect all publically-available information* and
2. *the price reaction to new information is unbiased*

The negative heuristic of the research programme forbids us to direct the modus tollens[73] at the hard core. Thus, the negative heuristic of the market efficiency programme can be stated in the following manner:

---

[72] Because the semi-strong form of the market efficiency hypothesis is considered to be the valid working hypothesis, I have chosen to let it represent the market efficiency hypothesis here. For further details, see Chapter 2.1.

[73] Se also note 43.

If the falsification of a statement or a prediction makes it necessary to revise or modify a part of the programme,[74] *then we should never hold the hard core (i.e., the two assumptions above) responsible for the falsification.*

Instead of holding the hard core responsible for the falsification, we should follow the directions given in the positive heuristic[75] of the research programme. The positive heuristic of the market efficiency programme can be very generally and formally stated in the following manner:

Any revision or modification of the research programme is done by changing or modifying assumptions of a theory/method or a theory/method itself within the protective belt.

In addition to this, the positive heuristic of the market efficiency research programme also consists of a number of more or less explicit rules or hints on how the theories and methods in the protective belt are revised or modified. When these are taken into account, the positive heuristic of the market efficiency research programme can be stated in the following and more specific manner:

1. Construct a method to test the hard core. Make the method's assumptions explicit.
2. Apply the method on empirical data.
3. If the test results are unfavorable, blame it on either the method or the data, e.g.,
   a) one or more of the test method's assumptions are more restrictive than the hard core demands ⇒ tailor, adjust or replace the method;[76]
   b) one or more of the assumptions used in the method for testing collide with the data:
   ⇒ develop new methods to deal with the data[77] or
   ⇒ discard/ignore the data.
4. If the test results are favorable, credit it to the hard core.
5. If new empirical observations are discovered as a bi-product of a test of the hard core:
   ⇒ develop new empirical theories to explain the discovery[78]
6. Test also these new empirical theories on empirical data, making sure to first make their assumptions as well as their predictions explicit. As these theories belong to the protective belt of the research programme, they are not immune to refutation although they will not be replaced before the emergence of a new and better theory within the protective belt

---

[74] For example, a theory or even a set of theories.

[75] Compare this with Lakatos (1970), p. 135:»...the positive heuristic consists of a partially articulated set of suggestions or hints on how to change, develop the »refutable variants« of the research-programme, how to modify, sophisticate, the »refutable« protective belt.«

[76] For example, the fact that the random walk model had more strict assumptions than the hard core demanded led to the development/sophistication of (new) methods for testing weak form efficiency.

[77] Look at the development of event study methodology for coping with event date and industry clustering and event-induced variance.

[78] The theories presented in Chapter 2.4 are an example of this, as they are created in an attempt to explain the price reaction observed in event studies focusing on acquisitions.

If empirical data collide with either the assumption(s) of the test, as referred to in (3b) or with the empirical theories, as referred to in (6), and the collision is not possible to explain within the research programme, the phenomenon will be labeled »an anomaly«. Anomalies will only influence theories and methods within the protective belt, and they will only be influenced to the extent the positive heuristic makes it possible to alter or replace them. Otherwise, anomalies will simply be ignored by the proponents of the research programme. In this respect, it is, however, important to acknowledge it takes time for the theories and methods within the protective belt to evolve.[79] So an anomaly that is ignored now may in the future be incorporated into the protective belt.[80]

Among the anomalies that the market efficiency research programme has not yet fully explained are »seasonal effects« and »the small firm effect«.[81] »Seasonal effects« comprise a number of anomalies for which a »seasonal« effect on stock returns is the common characteristic. This implies the market is inefficient. The »blue Monday effect« means that NYSE-stocks have a lower return on Mondays than on other days of the week.[82] The »January effect« or the »turn-of-the-year effect« means that stock returns on average are higher in January, i.e., at the turn of the year, than in other months. The »small firm effect« means that shares in small firms earn a larger return than do shares in general, for a given risk.[83]

There are, however, a number of previous anomalies for which adequate explanation has been provided in the protective belt of the research programme. The theories presented in the next section are examples of these.

---

79 This is also true for the hard core, as expressed by Lakatos (1978), p. 48fn:»The actual hard core of a programme does not actually emerge fully armed like Athene from the head of Zeus. It develops slowly, by a long, preliminary process of trial and error.«

80 The attitude toward anomalies described above is also very telling of the market efficiency research programme, as expressed by Elton & Gruber (1991), p.43: »We call them anomalies because we don't understand why they exist. We could view them as inefficiencies [of the efficient market research programme; author's note] or as evidence that we don't as yet completely understand equilibrium. If they are truly anomalies with no economic basis, then one would expect the very research we have described to draw sufficient attention to them that they will cease to exist.« And Jensen (1978), p. 100: »I have little doubt that in the next several years we will document further anomalies and begin to sort out and understand their causes. The result will not be an abandonment of the »efficiency« concept, nor of asset pricing models. Five years from now, however, we will as a profession have a much better understanding of these concepts than we now possess, and we will have a much more fundamental understanding of the world around us.«

81 The market's microstructure, i.e., its composition of market participants, has been suggested as a plausible explanation for some of the anomalies. For example, some investors may have a strong (tax) incentive to buy stocks at the end of the year.

82 See Smith (1990), p. 366+; Elton & Gruber (1991), p. 431; and Fama (1991), p. 1586+.

83 See Elton & Gruber (1991), p. 429.

3. The Protective Belt: Focus on Acquisition Theories

A large proportion of the empirical theories in the protective belt of the market efficiency research programme have evolved from chance discoveries produced by tests of the hard core. This has also been the case with respect to theories on acquisitions and the stock market's appraisal of acquisitions, which will be presented in this chapter.

In a vast amount of event studies,[84] the events studied have been acquisitions,[85] more specifically, domestic (especially U.S.) acquisitions. The event studies have examined price changes, i.e., changes in the shareholder value,[86] with respect to the acquiring companies' shareholders, as well as the acquired (target) companies' shareholders. The evidence of these studies show that, by far, the major proportion of shareholder value creation in acquisitions goes to the target's shareholders.

In their review of empirical studies on (U.S.) acquisitions, Jensen & Ruback (1983) conclude that target firm shareholders benefit from acquisitions, and shareholders do not lose - as measured by the stock market's reaction two days to one month after the acquisition announcement. But Jensen & Ruback (1983) also report that several studies show indications of systematic reductions in the stock prices of bidding firms in the year following the takeover. More recent studies[87] show that the change in the acquirers' shareholder value[88] following an acquisition has been declining by the decades since the 1960s, reaching negative, although statistically insignificant, changes in the 1980's.

This evidence of relatively small or negative returns to the acquirers's shareholders can be interpreted to mean that acquisitions on average are poor investments. But if acquisitions are poor investments, why are they undertaken?

Within the protective belt of the market efficiency research programme, there are two theories that address that question, namely, Jensen's »free cash flow hypothesis« and Roll's »hubris hypothesis«. Both these theories will be presented in the next two sections of this chapter. In addition to these two theories, there have been a number of more exploratory studies within the market efficiency research programme that have examined possible sources of shareholder value creation in foreign acquisitions. In order to fully account for the work done in the protective belt of the market

---

[84] That is, tests of the semi-strong form of the efficient market hypothesis. See Chapters 2.1.1 and 3.1.

[85] In the following review of the studies made on acquisitions, I do not distinguish between acquisitions, mergers and takeovers. Rather I use the term acquisition to cover them all.

[86] See footnote 52.

[87] For example, Bradley, Desai & Kim (1988) and Jarrell, Brickley & Netter (1988).

[88] Here, it is measured as cumulative abnormal returns (CAR) measured in the event studies. See Chapter 3.1.2 for further details about CAR.

efficiency research programme on acquisitions, these more exploratory studies will be presented in the final section of this chapter.

3.1. Jensen's Free Cash Flow Hypothesis

The »free cash flow hypothesis« by Jensen (1986a) is based on the efficient market hypothesis as well as agency theory. As Jensen (1986b) puts it, it is central to the »free cash flow hypothesis« that:[89]

> »Managers are the agent of shareholders, and because both parties are self-interested, there are serious conflicts between them over the choice of the best corporate strategy. Agency costs are the total costs that arise in such cooperative arrangements.«

Resting on the assumption that managers act in their own interest, the »free cash flow hypothesis« further postulates that managers with access to free cash flow[90] will prefer to spend this cash flow on investments, at their own discretion, instead of distributing the cash flow as a dividend. If free cash flow is defined as that which is left when all profitable investment possibilities are used up, the investments made with free cash flow will per definition be poor investments. Thus, the »free cash flow hypothesis« sees the negative returns to acquirers' shareholders as agency costs,[91] costs that occur because managers act in their own self-interest and not in the interest of their shareholders. But this does not mean that the theory only holds a negative view of acquisitions. On the contrary, the market for corporate control[92] serves as a regulating force for agency costs when the shareholders do not have the necessary control of their managers actions. So when agency costs are high, e.g., due to bad acquisitions, the acquiring company will be a potential target itself, as another company can make a good investment by acquiring the company and replacing the management for running the company in a more efficient way.

---

[89] p. 12.

[90] Jensen (1986a) defines free cash flow as: »cash flow in excess of that required to fund all projects that have positive net present values when discounted at the relevant cost of capital.« p. 323.

[91] According to Jensen (1986a), agency cost consists of: »..the costs of monitoring managerial behavior (such as the cost of producing audited financial statements and devising and implementing compensation plans that reward managers for actions that increase investors' wealth) and the inevitable costs that are incurred because the conflicts of interest can never be resolved perfectly.« p. 12. The agency cost referred to here is of the last sort.

[92] The market for corporate control refers to the (stock) market as a mechanism for monitoring and regulating agency cost due to the separation of ownership and control. As such, it relies on the efficient market hypothesis. It assumes a high negative correlation between agency cost and the stock price of a specific company. So high agency cost, e.g., due to managerial inefficiency and lack of ownership control, will lead the stock price to decline and thereby make the company a potential acquisition target.

The »free cash flow hypothesis« makes several empirical predictions relevant for acquisitions. Using Jensen (1986a), they can be listed as:[93]

1. »...managers of firms with unused borrowing power and large free cash flows are more likely to undertake low-benefit or even value-destroying mergers.«
2. »In declining industries, mergers within the industry will create value, and mergers outside the industry are more likely to be low- or even negative-return projects.«
3. »The theory predicts value increasing takeovers occur in response to breakdowns of internal control processes in firms with substantial free cash flow and organizational policies (including diversification programs) that are wasting resources.«
4. »Targets will be of two kinds: firms with poor management that have done poorly prior to the merger, and firms that have done exceptionally well and have large free cash flow which they refuse to pay out to shareholders«
5. »Acquisitions not made with stock involve payout of resources to (target) shareholders and this can create net benefits even if the merger generates operating inefficiencies.«[94]
6. »..free cash flow theory predicts that many acquirers will tend to have exceptionally good performance prior to acquisition. ...That exceptional performance generates the free cash flow for the acquisition.«

Of the empirical predictions of the »free cash flow hypothesis« given above, five of them can be tested by examining the size of the free cash flow of acquirers, targets and other (i.e., bench-mark) companies. Predictions 1 to 3 all specify which type of acquisitions will create and destroy value, respectively, and predictions 4 and 6 specify the characteristics of target firms and »many«[95] acquirers. To the extent it is possible to measure or to approximate free cash flow, it is also possible to test predictions 1, 2, 3, 4 and 6.

Studies testing these predictions have most commonly used Tobin's q[96] as an estimate of whether a firm has access to investment projects having a positive net present value, i.e., free cash flow. If firms have investment projects with a positive

---

[93] p. 328.

[94] Jensen (1986a) uses the terms »acquisitions«, »mergers« and »takeovers« interchangeably. Thus, it is not a typing error that »acquisitions« and »merger« are used interchangeably in the quotation.

[95] That is, the acquirers who make value-destroying acquisitions.

[96] Tobin's q is the ratio of the firm's market value to its replacement cost. As not all companies report replacement cost, book value is used as a rough approximation. When book value is used instead of replacement cost, then Tobin's q is equal to the Danish »kurs/indre værdi«.There are, however, problems in using »kurs/indre værdi« on Danish data to test the prediction of the »free cash flow hypothesis«. For further details, see Chapter 3.2.1.

net present value, then their q will be larger than 1. If not, their q will be less than 1.[97] In their study on the gains from successful domestic (U.S.) tender offers, Lang, Stultz & Walkling (1989) found that:[98]

»...the shareholders of high q bidders gain significantly more than the shareholders of low q bidders. In general, the shareholders of low q targets benefit more from takeovers than the shareholders of high q targets. Typical bidders have persistently low q ratios prior to the acquisition announcement while target q decline significantly over the five years before the tender offer.«

Thus, the Lang, Stulz & Walkling study strongly supports the predictions of the »free cash flow hypothesis« to the degree Tobin's q is a good approximation of free cash flow. In a similar study, Servaes (1991) confirmed the results of Lang, Stulz & Walkling, but on a larger sample, which includes both domestic (U.S.) mergers and tender offers.

Prediction 5 specifies the advantages of paying cash instead of exchanging shares for a target. This prediction can be tested by comparing the value creation in acquisitions paid for with cash and with stock, respectively. In his study cf. above, Servaes (1991) confirms this prediction and reports that:[99]

»...both targets and bidder have larger abnormal return in all-cash takeovers. In fact, total returns are 10% larger in cash takeovers than in pure securities takeovers. Another interesting finding is that total returns are actually negative in an exchange of securities.«

In all, it may be concluded that the studies testing the predictions of the »free cash flow hypothesis« have been quite affirmative, although limited in number. To my knowledge, there have been no studies testing the predictions of the »free cash flow hypothesis« on foreign acquisitions.

3.2. Roll's Hubris Hypothesis

Another explanation of why acquisitions are undertaken even if they are not associated with any gains is the »hubris hypothesis« proposed by Roll (1986). The »hubris hypothesis« simply states that if there actually are no gains associated with the acquisition, then the acquisition is caused by hubris on the part of the acquiring company's decision makers: they simply believe that they can estimate the true value of the target better than the market; but in reality, they have just overestimated the target and/or the acquisition gains.

---

[97] Note: there will be differences in the size of Tobin's q among different industries. For example, it would be expected that the q for service industries will, in general, be higher than that for production industries.

[98] p. 137.

[99] p. 413.

As Roll notes, the »hubris hypothesis« is consistent with strong form market efficiency, but: [100]

». . . even if gains do exist for some corporate combinations,[101] at least part of the average observed takeover premium could still be caused by valuation error and hubris.«

Assuming there are no gains associated with acquisitions, then, according to Roll (1986), the »hubris hypothesis« predicts that:[102]

»...the average increase in the target firm's market value should then be more than offset by the average decrease in the value of the bidding firm. Takeover expenses would constitute the aggregate net loss. The market price of a target firm should increase when a previously unanticipated bid is announced.... Implications for the market price reaction of a bidding firm are somewhat less clear. If we could be sure that *(a)* the bid was unanticipated and *(b)* the bid conveys no information about the bidder other than that it is seeking a combination with a particular target, then the hubris hypothesis would predict the following market price movement in bidding firms:
1. a price decline on announcement of a bid;
2. a price increase on abandoning a bid or on losing a bid; and
3. a price decline on actually winning a bid.«

The empirical studies partly support the »hubris hypothesis«. There is clear evidence that acquisitions create shareholder value for the target's shareholders.[103] However, evidence also indicates that the acquirers' shareholders do not lose.[104] Even if the acquirers' shareholder value has been declining throughout the decades since the 1960's, it is first in the 1980's that studies have reported negative - although statistically insignificant - changes in shareholder value.[105] Thus, despite the predictions of the »hubris hypothesis«, it seems that there is empirical support for some aggregated gains associated with acquisitions.

Furthermore, Roll argues that the lack of recurring acquisition decisions in managers' careers is the reason why they do not account properly for the »winner's

---

[100] Roll (1986) says that: »Financial markets are assumed to be efficient in that asset prices reflect all information about individual firms. Product and labor markets are assumed efficient in the sense that *(a)* no industrial reorganization can bring gains in an aggregate output at the same cost or reductions in aggregate costs with the same output and *(b)* management is employed in its best alternate use.« p. 200.

[101] This is equivalent to semi-strong efficiency, i.e., the presence of synergies and insider information can cause the value of the target to be higher than the present market value of the target for the acquirer.

[102] p. 201.

[103] See Jensen & Ruback (1983).

[104] See Jensen & Ruback (1983).

[105] See Bradley, Desai & Kim (1988) and Jarrell, Brickley & Netter (1988).

curse.« However, one might expect managers to learn from other managers' experience, that is, from empirical studies examining acquisitions. Apparently, this would have not been the case if the »hubris hypothesis« were taken as given, as in the studies[106] showing declining takeover gains to the acquirers throughout the decades and thus implying that managers' acquisition decisions have been increasingly affected by hubris. All in all, empirical support for the »hubris hypothesis« is mixed.

3.3. Exploratory Studies on International Acquisitions and Shareholder Value Creation

Although there has only been a limited number of studies on foreign acquisitions, there are indications of more positive wealth gains associated with foreign acquisitions than with their domestic counterparts. In the following, a number of exploratory studies on acquisitions and shareholder wealth creation will be presented. Their common characteristic is that they all explore possible explanatory determinants of shareholder wealth rather than test a fully-developed theory.

Markides & Ittner (1994) found that international acquisitions on average created value for the acquiring firms[107] and that wealth creation in their sample was a function of the acquisition's relatedness, the concentration level and advertising intensity in the acquirer's industry, the acquirer's previous international experience, and current profitability along with the nature of the macroeconomic environment, i.e., tax regulations and the relative strength of the U.S. dollar. But surprisingly, they also found that a single variable, SIZE, defined as the target's sales divided by the acquirer's sales in the year of the acquisition, could explain about 25% of the value creation in their subsample.[108]

In their study of 301 foreign acquisitions made by U.S. companies, Doukas & Travlos (1988) found that acquisitions were associated with positive returns to the acquirers' shareholders in those cases where the acquirer did not operate in the target's home country before the acquisition.[109] On average, however, they did not find any wealth effects - positive nor negative - associated with foreign acquisitions. Quite interestingly, they also showed that returns to the acquirers' shareholders were

---

[106] Bradley, Desai & Kim (1988) and Jarrell, Brickley & Netter (1988).

[107] The $CAR_{(t=-1,0)}$= 0.32% and the t-statistic is 1.89 (significant at the 10% level or lower). For further details about CAR, see Chapter 3.1.2.

[108] The SIZE data was only available for 83 of the 276 acquisitions included in Markides & Ittner's study. The average adjusted R^2 was 13 % before the inclusion of SIZE in the regressions, but more than 40% after SIZE was included in the regressions.

[109] These acquisitions had an $AR_{t=0}$=0.31% (z-value = 2.11) which is significant at the 5% level in a one-tailed test as opposed to an $AR_{t=0}$ = 0.08% (z-value = 0.84) for the total sample.

larger when the target was located in a less developed country[110] - perhaps an effect of low competition in the host country.

In all, it seems like foreign acquisitions create relatively more value for the acquirer's shareholders than domestic acquisitions do. Interestingly, this also seems to be the case for the shareholders of the target companies. In their comparative study of domestic and foreign acquisitions using data from the U.S. stock market, Harris & Ravenscraft (1991) found that U.S. targets in foreign acquisitions had significantly higher wealth gains than U.S. targets in domestic acquisitions. While the wealth gains were not well explained by industry and tax variables, the weakness of the U.S. dollar was positively related to wealth gains.

4. Assessment of the Market Efficiency Research Programme

The market efficiency research programme has been quite successful in protecting its hard core. Over the years, the hard core has been developed from the initial market efficiency hypothesis to the current version where the second of three forms, i.e., the semi-strong form, and the assumption of an unbiased price reaction now constitutes the hard core of the research programme and also the dominant working hypothesis within the area of finance.

Within the protective belt of the research programme, a massive number of theories and methods have evolved. However, this chapter has mainly dealt with those focusing on acquisitions. If the market efficiency research programme is assessed only by the theories and methods presented in this chapter, then it will be assessed as stagnating because all of the theories are post hoc explanations of empirical observations, i.e., the theoretical growth of the market efficiency research programme is lagging behind its empirical growth. However, the market efficiency research programme is in no immediate danger of being rejected,[111] being the most dominant research programme in the area of finance, with no apparent rival programme.

[110] In the cross sectional regression analysis on the entire sample, the dummy variable representing the degree of economic development in the target's country (less developed = 1) was positive and significant at the 1% level. The explanatory power of the regressions on the entire sample ranged from R^2 = 3.10% to R^2 = 3.54%.

[111] A research programme is rejected when the work on it ceases cf. Lakatos (1970), p.157n.

CHAPTER 3

Testing the Market Efficiency Research Programme: The Danish Stock Market's Appraisal of Danish International Acquisitions 1988-1992

In this chapter the market efficiency research programme is tested. More specifically two tests (or sets of tests) are conducted.

The first set of tests examines - to the extent possible with the available data - whether the theories of acquisitions in the protective belt are valid for Danish stock market data with respect to Danish foreign acquisitions between 1988 and 1992. The test methodology, i.e., the event study methodology, used for this first test is presented in the first section of this chapter - both in a non-technical and technical manner. In the next section of this chapter, the first set of tests is conducted. These include different tests of the predictions of the theories of acquisitions in the protective belt.

The second set of tests examines the validity of the unbiasedness hypothesis of the market efficiency research programme, i.e., whether the event study's appraisal of acquisitions was correct. The method applied and the data and the results of the second set of tests are presented in the third section of this chapter.

The final section of this chapter presents the theoretical implications of the two set of tests.

1. The Event Study Methodology

This chapter presents the event study methodology. In the first section of this chapter, the concept of the event study methodology is presented in a non-technical way. The purpose is to illustrate the possibilities and the limitations of event studies, including those which might be especially relevant to the Danish stock market. The second section of this chapter accounts for the formulas and test statistics that are to be used in the event study conducted in Chapter 3.2.

1.1. Introduction to the Event Study Methodology

Event study is the generic term for several models used in evaluating the effect of specific types of events (e.g., acquisitions, regulations, the release of annual reports) on the stock price and thus shareholders' wealth. In the following treatment of assumptions, limitations, and use of the event study methodology, the focus will be of one of the models, the so-called market model.[112] The market model is, by far, the most used model in event studies, mainly because the market model and its test statistics are well-specified for a variety of conditions,[113] and also because most of the assumptions are identical. Regardless of the specific model used, the choice to focus solely on the market model seem justified.

To fully understand event study methodology, it is crucial also to understand the concept of (stock) market efficiency.[114] For the purpose of explaining market efficiency, envision the stock market as a transformer. For a given listed company, the stock market transforms all relevant information into the stock price. The individual market participants may have different interpretations of the information and thus different expectations, but the transforming process converges these into a market consensus price.

This also implies that it is possible for individual investors to have irrational expectations and act (i.e., sell or buy) accordingly. But because there are many market participants, irrational expectations will be eliminated either because there are also irrational expectations in the opposite direction or because people with rational expectations will take advantage of the disequilibrium caused by irrational expectations. The length of time it takes to eliminate irrational expectations will vary with the number of market participants and the amount of capital the individual market participants have.

If the market participants expect new information to be relevant for a given listed company, then the market will react with price changes. The concept of market efficiency is concerned with the speed with which the market incorporates new information, i.e., what actually can be regarded as »new« information. When it is not possible to earn money on historical information,[115] then the market is said to be weak form efficient. If it is not possible to earn money by acting on any public information, then the market is said to be semi-strong form efficient. Finally, if it is not possible to earn money on any information - published or insider, the market is said to be strong form efficient.

---

[112] The market model is sometimes also called the OLS market model.

[113] Se Brown & Warner (1985) and Brown & Warner (1980) for an examination of the power of four different event study models when daily and weekly stock returns are used, respectively.

[114] See Chapter 2.2, which presents the market efficiency hypothesis in a more technical way.

[115] Studies show that it is normally a matter of days before new information is incorporated into the price and subsequently becomes »historical«.

The idea of event studies is basically to study price changes on the day that new information is made public and on the days surrounding that announcement.[116] The event study methodology assumes semi-strong efficiency,[117] i.e., it assumes that all public information is already incorporated in the price; and if any new information is made public, then the market will react swiftly with price changes if and only if the market expects this information to have an impact on shareholder value. This also implies that, if the market does not react with price changes, there are three possible causes for this, namely:

1) the market does not expect the information to have any effect on the shareholder value,
2) it is not *new* information, or
3) the market is strong form efficient.

Normally, point 3) is discarded.[118]

When we want to focus solely on the effects of a specific piece or type of information on shareholder wealth, it is necessary, as far as possible, to eliminate any other information that might affect the price. This is normally done in two ways in event studies. First, the event window has to be clean of all new information other than the item being analyzed.[119] Second, using the market model, the calculated »return« is adjusted for general market movements, inflation and the specific company's market risk. What is left after this adjustment is, in fact, the *abnormal* return.

The abnormal return is the central measure in event studies. Because any irrelevant information has been removed from the period being analyzed, the abnormal return measures the market's (i.e., the investors' and owners') *expectations* of the effect of a specific event on shareholder value. The abnormal return can be calculated for an individual company or a sample of companies.[120] In the latter case possible company-specific effects of the event are reduced.

---

[116] The days on which price changes are studied are normally referred to as the *event window*.

[117] Event study methodology is, in fact, in itself *also* a test of semi-strong efficiency; i.e., it is both a test of the effects of an event and a test of semi-strong market efficiency.

[118] In some event studies, stock prices have been shown to change before the information has been made public (see e.g., Sørensen (1982)), implying that someone is trading on insider information. If this is the case, strong form efficiency is rejected. Note that significant, abnormal price changes before the publication of new information could also be caused by pure speculation, e.g., before the release of annual report announcements.

[119] Some researchers extend the clean data period to include the estimation period for some types of information, e.g., additional acquisitions. But because this has important implications for the representativity of the sample and, as most researchers agree that stock markets incorporate new information fairly quickly, the clean data period is normally equal to the event window.

[120] Thus, it is referred to as the average abnormal return.

The sign of the abnormal return will indicate if the market expects the new information to be positive or negative for shareholder value. The size of the abnormal return depends on the expected economic impact on shareholders' wealth, as well as the degree to which the market is surprised by the information, i.e., considers the information news.

The stock market's expectations are assumed to be unbiased because it is not possible to earn money by acting on new information.[121] That the expectations are unbiased does not mean that the market cannot be wrong in its expectations, but rather that these wrong expectations are just as often positive as they are negative. For the same reason, the average abnormal return (AR) is often seen as a performance measure. In this respect, it is important once again to emphase that AR only measures the market's expectations with respect to the event and not the actual performance.

There are several advantages in using AR as a performance measure. First, stock prices are the only direct measure of shareholder value; and by using these in the calculation of AR, it is possible to enlighten the expectations of an important group of stakeholders, namely the owners. Furthermore, stock prices have several desirable features:[122] they are fully specified,[123] they are readily available for all publically-traded companies,[124] they are reported objectively, and they are not as easy for managers to manipulate as, for example, accounting figures are.

But there are also disadvantages when using the event study methodology. First and foremost, AR as a performance measure is limited in its focus to one group of stakeholders: the investors, or more specifically, the fully diversified investor. Considering the ownership structure on the Danish stock market,[125] this focus can be somewhat problematic. A large proportion of Danish companies listed on the Danish stock exchange maintain dual voting classes of shares, where an A-share typically has ten votes and a B-share has only one vote. Furthermore, the proportion of A-shares to B-shares is often constructed in a way that gives the A-shares the voting majority. This is important as the A-shares are often held by the founder, the heirs of the founder or a foundation, and thus are not in circulation. So owners of the B-shares - in principle the fully diversified investor, which the event study methodology focuses on - only represent a proportion of the owners. Moreover, the

---

[121] This is an implication of the semi-strong form of the market efficiency hypothesis. See also Chapter 2.2.

[122] See Lubatkin & Shrieves (1986) for an extended discussion of the advantages of using stock prices and AR as a performance measure.

[123] That is, stock prices are not limited to a single aspect of performance, such as a change in profit or sales, but rather they measure all possible informational aspects of performance.

[124] Thus, it is also both easy and possible to compare two competitors.

[125] See Stonehill & Dullum (1990) and Strandskov, Thomsen & Pedersen (1994) for studies on the characteristics of the ownership structure of Danish Companies.

owners of A-shares will often have most of their wealth tied up in the A-shares (i.e., in a single company), and thus have a preference for a stable and secure yield (i.e., income) on their shares. But if an investor only holds a single stock, his risk will be much higher than that for the fully diversified investor, and his income will be more unstable and insecure. The owners of A-shares might, therefore, have an interest in getting the company to diversify and thereby reduce the risks. This creates a possible conflict of interests between the owners of the A-shares and the B-shares, respectively. On the other hand, the tight control that owners of A-shares often have over management can reduce the agency cost of the company.[126]

Another problem with event study methodology is that some types of events, e.g., an acquisition, might change the company's market risk.[127] When the risk of a stock changes, the return is also expected to change, implying that an AR - or at least a part of it - may be caused by a risk adjustment. In order to overcome this potential problem, the AR is normally calculated using two different estimation periods - a pre-event estimation period and a pre-and-post-event estimation period. A check is made to see if there are significant differences in the two calculated AR's.

Summarizing, there are both limitations and advantages to using event studies. But as long as the assumptions of event study methodology are kept in mind when making conclusions about the results, event study methodology is a good tool for enlightening the expectations of one group of stakeholders, the fully diversified shareholders, about the effect of management's decisions on shareholder value.

1.2. The Model for Estimation of the Abnormal Return and the Test Statistics

In this section, the definitions and test statistics used in the event study conducted on the Danish stock market will be developed.

The data used for the empirical study are the daily stock prices for companies listed on the Danish stock exchange during the period July, 1, 1987-March 31, 1993,[128] as compiled in the database »BØRSDATABASEN«, available at the Aarhus School of Business. The price data used are not raw data, but pseudo-data corrected for dividend and new issues that are readily available in the database.

The rate of return on security *j* for event day *t* is defined by:

$$(1)\ R_{j,t} = \ln[\frac{P_{j,t}}{P_{j,t-k}}]^{1/k}$$

---

[126] Strandskov, Thomsen & Pedersen (1994) conclude in their study that companies owned (i.e., controlled) by families or foundations seem to be performing slightly better - measured on a numbers of economic (accounting) performance measures - than companies with a diffused ownership structure; p. 10.

[127] The company's market risk is the β in equation (2) in Chapter 3.1.2.

[128] This period extends the analyzed period, January, 1, 1988- December, 31, 1992, with the necessary pre- and post-acquisition estimation periods.

where:

t :	the number of trading days on the Copenhagen Stock Exchange relative to the announcement day (t=0) in Børsen
$P_{j,t}$:	the price of security j on day t, corrected for dividend and new issues
$P_{j,t-k}$:	the price of security j on day $t-k$ corrected for dividend and new issues
k :	the number of trading days between two quotes.

$R_{j,t}$ expresses the return on the security when interest rates are compounded. Furthermore, the rate of return is adjusted for non-trading days. If there is more than one day between the quotes, then the daily rate of return is determined as an average given the number of days. Some of the stocks traded on the Copenhagen Stock Exchange are traded rather infrequently. An effect of this infrequent trading could be large - positive or negative - returns if the correction is not made, thus implying high volatility rather than merely the effects of a longer period between trades. On these grounds, the choice was made to adjust for non-trading days in the calculation of the return.[129]

An estimate of the value of the security's returns in the absence of an acquisition (that is, a control return) is needed to calculate the abnormal return for a security. This study uses the market model[130] to calculate the control return. Thus, the control return on security j on day t is defined as:

$$(2)\ CR_{j,t} = \hat{\alpha}_j - \hat{\beta}_j \cdot R_{m,t}$$

where:

$R_{m,t}$:	the return on the market portfolio for day t
$\hat{\alpha}_j$, $\hat{\beta}_j$:	parameters estimated when regressing the individual security's return $R_{j,t}$, on the market return, $R_{m,t}$, for the estimation period[131]

[129] This will not have any effect on abnormal returns or cumulative abnormal returns calculated in the event window due to the additional criterion, that the security has to be traded on each of the days included in the event window and on the day immediately before the event window begins. See Chapter 3.2.2.

[130] The market model simply states that the relationship between $R_{j,t}$ and $R_{m,t}$ can be expressed as:

$$R_{j,t} = \hat{\alpha}_j + \hat{\beta}_j \cdot R_{m,t} + \hat{\epsilon}_j \ .$$

[131] The estimation period is: t = [-124;-6].

For any security j, the abnormal return[132] for event day t is defined as:[133]

$$(3)\ AR_{j,t} = R_{j,t} - CR_{j,t}$$

Assuming that the individual abnormal return is normally and independently distributed across securities, the test statistic, t_t, under the null hypothesis that the average abnormal return on day t, ($\overline{AR_t}$), is equal to zero, is:

$$(4)\ t_t = \overline{AR_t} \,/\, \hat{S}(\overline{AR_t}) \sim t(N-1)$$

where:

$$\overline{AR_t} = \frac{1}{N} \cdot \sum_{j=1}^{N} AR_{j,t}$$

$$\hat{S}(\overline{AR_t}) = \sqrt{\sum_{t=-124}^{t=-6} (\overline{AR_t} - \overline{\overline{AR}})^2 \,/\, (T-1)}$$

$$\overline{\overline{AR}} = \frac{1}{T} \cdot \sum_{t=-124}^{t=-6} (\overline{AR_t})$$

and N : number of acquisitions in the sample
T : number of days for which the stock has been quoted in the estimation period.

The robustness of the results is checked by performing a binomial sign test in addition to the test shown in equation (4). Because the binomial sign test is a test of location, it will not be affected by the sizes of the abnormal return. When conducting the binomial sign test, the significance of the results are found via tables of cumulative binomial distributions.

In some instances, it can be relevant to study the possible differences in the AR's of different subsamples, e.g., to examine if the stock market reacts more positively to the acquisitions of some types of companies. The daily mean difference between the average abnormal returns of samples x and y, respectively, is defined as:

---

[132] Note that $AR_{j,t}$ is equivalent to the residual, $\hat{\epsilon}_{j,t}$, in the market model.

[133] The test statistic, under the null hypothesis that $AR_{j,t} = 0$, is:

$$t_{j,t} = AR_{j,t} \,/\, \hat{S}(AR_{j,t})\ ;$$

where

$$\hat{S}(AR_{j,t}) = \sqrt{\sum_{t=-124}^{t=-6} (AR_{j,t} - \overline{AR_j})^2 \,/\, (T-1)} \quad \text{and} \quad \overline{AR_j} = \frac{1}{T} \sum_{t=-124}^{t=-6} AR_{j,t}$$

$$(5)\quad DAR_t = \overline{AR}_{x,t} - \overline{AR}_{y,t}$$

The test statistic *D*, under the null hypothesis that DAR_t is equal to zero, is:

$$(6)\quad D = \frac{DAR_t}{\hat{s}_j \cdot \sqrt{\frac{1}{N_x} + \frac{1}{N_y}}} \sim t\,(N_x + N_y - 2)$$

where:

$$\hat{s}_j = \sqrt{\frac{\hat{S}^2(\overline{AR}_{x,t})\cdot(N_x - 1) + \hat{S}^2(\overline{AR}_{y,t})\cdot(N_y - 1)}{(N_x + N_y - 2)}}$$

and:

N_x : the number of acquisitions in sample *x*
N_y : the number of acquisitions in sample *y*.

This study has relied on reports in the Danish business newspaper, *Børsen*, to identify announcements of acquisition activity. Using this approach makes it a problem to identify the specific trading day on which the news reached the market. That is, was the news familiar to the market on the day the newspaper published the announcement (t=0) or on the day before (t=-1). To take this into account, the cumulative abnormal return (CAR) is studied. The CAR for the sample on day *t* is defined as:

$$(7)\quad CAR_{(t=-1,0)} = \frac{1}{N}\sum_{j=1}^{N}\sum_{t=-1}^{t=0} AR_{j,t}$$

The test statistic *Q*, under the null hypothesis that $CAR_{(t=-1,0)}$ is equal to zero, is:

$$(8)\quad Q = \frac{\sqrt{N}\cdot CAR_{(t=-1,0)}}{\hat{s}\,(CAR)} \sim t\,(N-1)$$

where:

$$\hat{s}(CAR) = \sqrt{P}\cdot \hat{s}(AR_t)$$

and

P : number of days in the CAR period.

2. The First Test: An Event Study of the Danish Stock Market's Appraisal of Danish International Acquisitions 1988-1992

The first subsection of this section presents the specific hypotheses tested later in this chapter. This second subsection presents the data that has been collected on Danish foreign acquisitions in the period 1988-1992 and shows how the initial sample had to be narrowed down in to meet the assumptions, etc. prescribed by event study methodology. The next section presents the results of the event study conducted on the reduced sample, using the formulas and test statistics presented in Chapter 3.1.2. The conclusions of the first test are presented in the final section of this chapter.

2.1. Developing the Hypothesis

The dominant research question in the literature on acquisitions has been whether acquisitions create shareholder value. This question is also addressed by theories within the market efficiency research programme.[134] Roll's »hubris hypothesis« is the most restrictive theory in this respect as it postulates that acquiring companies' shareholders lose shareholder value upon an acquisition announcement.[135] Jensen's »free cash flow hypothesis« is less restrictive as it postulates that acquiring companies' shareholders only lose shareholder value upon an acquisition announcement if the acquiring companies have unused borrowing power and large free cash flows.[136]

This book addresses the research question whether acquisitions create shareholder value or not using event study methodology, a methodology that is embedded in the market efficiency research programme. When event study methodology is employed to test the effects of an event on shareholder value, it is important to realize this is not only a test of effects on shareholder value, but also a test of the stock market's efficiency under the joint hypothesis that the market model is the correct pricing model for the stock market. However, this last part will be ignored in the presentation of the empirical results in Chapter 3.2.3 because the focus of this book is on acquisitions and not on market efficiency. Therefore, it will simply be assumed that the Danish stock market is semi-strong efficient.[137]

---

134 See Chapter 2.3.

135 Or more specifically:»...the hubris hypothesis would predict the following market price movement in bidding firms: 1. a price decline on announcement of a bid...« Roll (1986), p. 201.

136 Or more specifically: »...managers of firms with unused borrowing power and large free cash flows are more likely to undertake low-benefit or even value-destroying mergers.« Jensen (1986a), p. 328.

137 The joint hypothesis that the Danish stock market is semi-strong efficient and that the market model is the correct pricing model herein is supported by the results in Chapter 3.2.3. Similarly, Lønroth & Reeb (1994) also found support of this hypothesis.

Using Roll's predictions as a basis, the specific hypothesis to be tested is formulated as follows:

H1: *The foreign acquisitions made in the period 1988-1992 by Danish companies listed on the Copenhagen Stock Exchange do* not *create shareholder value for the acquiring companies' shareholders.*

H1 will be tested on the total sample and on two different sets of subsamples (representing different frequencies of acquisition activity [138] and different types of ownership, both of the acquiring company,[139] respectively) using different measures of shareholder value (AR and CAR[140]).

An important implication of semi-strong market efficiency is that information that is not new to the market will not be expected to have any price effect. Similarly, if acquisitions made by frequent/ experienced acquirers are (partly) expected by the market, then price reactions would not be expected (or the price reactions would be of a more corrective nature).[141] The subsamples representing different frequencies of acquisition activity are created to test if »acquisition frequency« is of importance to shareholder value. It should be noted that this hypothesis (that »acquisition frequency« is of importance to shareholder value) is not a competing hypothesis with either that posited by Roll and or that posited by Jensen. Rather it is a hypothesis that should be tested before those of Roll and Jensen because support of Roll's and Jensen's hypotheses, i.e., an acceptance of hypothesis H1 for the total sample, would otherwise be undermined if the »acquisition frequency«-hypothesis was supported subsequently.

As mentioned in Chapter 3.1.1, the ownership structure of companies listed on the Copenhagen Stock Exchange has a special feature, namely the wide use of dual voting classes of shares, which makes it possible for a relatively small group of owners to control the company. The effects of this ownership structure is ambiguous. The controlling shareholders may take advantage of their position and make diversifying acquisitions,[142] for example. But on the other hand, they may also be able to control management more tightly and subsequently reduce agency cost, which otherwise would occur. To test the effects of ownership structure on the stock market's reaction, i.e., shareholder value, to the acquisition announcements, the total

---

[138] »Major acquirers« and »other acquirers«. See Chapter 3.2.2 for further details.

[139] »Family ownership«, »foundation ownership« and »diversified ownership«. See Chapter 3.2.2.

[140] See Chapter 3.1 for further details about these measures.

[141] See Chapter 3.1.1, page 47, point 3).

[142] Diversifying acquisitions are normally not considered advantageous because the investor is able to diversify his/her portfolio if he/she desires to do so. The disadvantage, in terms of shareholder value, of diversifying acquisitions, as opposed to taking on related acquisitions, is supported by most recent studies. See Morck et al. (1990).

sample has been divided into three subsamples, each representing a specific type of ownership.[143]

Finally, in order to examine the significance of the difference in the AR between different subsamples, the following hypothesis will be tested:

H2: *There is a difference in the changes in shareholder value following the announcement of foreign acquisitions made during the period 1988-1992 by Danish companies listed on the Copenhagen Stock Exchange with respect to acquirer's »acquisition frequency« and the type of ownership of the acquiring company.*

If the test of H1 shows that shareholder value is created upon the acquisition announcement, then Roll's »hubris hypothesis« can be rejected with respect to this data. However, it is not possible to reject Jensen's »free cash flow hypothesis« solely on the proof of shareholder value creation. In order to reject Jensen's »free cash flow hypothesis« with respect to this data, it is necessary to take the size of the acquiring companies' free cash flow into account. As mentioned in Chapter 2.3.1, this is normally done via the use of Tobin's *q* - an indication of the size of the free cash flow. However, this is not possible with this data due to Danish accounting legislation, according to which Danish companies are allowed to - and widely do[144] - depreciate the goodwill of acquired companies[145] immediately over equity.[146] When goodwill is depreciated in this manner, it will result in a fall in the book value and, subsequently, a higher *q* when book value is used as an approximation of the replacement costs, as is done by most studies. Because the effect will be a rise in *q*, regardless of whether the investment is considered good or not by the stock market, it would not be a good measure to test Jensen's »free cash flow hypothesis« on Danish data.

Furthermore, it is not possible to examine the predictions of Jensen's »free cash flow hypothesis« and Roll's »hubris hypothesis« regarding the change in shareholder value of *target* companies because the relevant data is available.[147] It has neither been possible to examine possible differences in shareholder value created for all-cash versus stock acquisitions because this data is not available.

---

[143] See Chapter 3.1.1 for further details about the subsamples.

[144] See Elling & Christiansen (1993), pp. 131-134.

[145] That is, the actual price paid for the acquired company less its book value.

[146] This form of depreciation is not allowed in U.S. accounting legislation.

[147] »Børsdatabasen« only gives access to Danish stock market data. Furthermore, some of the targets are not listed companies. See also Chapter 5.2.1, Table 5.3, Question 1.2.

2.2. The Data

The sphere of interest in this book is Danish foreign acquisitions made over the five-year period, January 1, 1988-December 31, 1992. However, the book only studies a subsample of Danish foreign acquisitions made in this period. This subsection describes the process by which the initial sample of Danish foreign acquisitions was narrowed down to the sample used in conducting the event study, along with some characteristics of the subsamples.

In Denmark, there are no public, periodic statistics on Danish foreign acquisitions; to establish the population, it has been necessary to look through all the issues of Børsen[148] published over the five-year period, as well as some other public sources that were screened in a more casual way. Initially, 233 acquisitions were identified as satisfying the following criteria:[149]

(1) the acquiring company was Danish or a subsidiary[150] of a Danish company, and
(2) a majority holding of the target was acquired.[151]

This initial sample is shown in Table 3.1.

[148] *Børsen* is the Danish equivalent of *The Wall Street Journal.*

[149] By far, the largest proportion of the acquisition announcement identified are announcements of acquisitions already agreed upon by the target and the acquirer. This could be an indication of preferences by Danish companies for quiet and friendly acquisitions.

[150] A subsidiary is defined as a company where another company directly or indirectly controls more than 50% of the voting power or has the right to appoint or remove a majority of the members of this enterprise. Thus, this definition also includes acquisitions made by Rentokil Group PLC, UK, which is a subsidiary of Sophus Berendsen A/S, DK.

[151] That is, the equity acquired would give the acquiring company control of 50% or more of the target company's voting power.

Table 3.1: The initial sample of Danish foreign acquisitions, by country, 1988-1992

Country	1988	1989	1990	1991	1992	1988-1992	
	---numbers of acquisitions---						% of total
U.K.	6	13	18	11	9	57	24
U.S.	9	7	8	5	5	34	15
Germany	8	8	5	9	4	34	15
Sweden	2	12	2	3	8	27	12
Norway	3	5	3	3	3	17	7
France	1	4	5	0	5	15	6
Netherlands	2	5	0	2	2	11	5
Finland	0	1	3	2	4	10	4
Others	0	7	6	9	6	28	12
Total	31	62	50	44	46	233	100

The approach used to collect the initial sample is not an ideal approach. That is, the sample does not include all Danish foreign acquisitions made. Furthermore, the sample is probably biased towards the larger acquisitions made by large companies and companies listed on the Copenhagen Stock Exchange,[152] as these are most likely of greatest interest to the readers of Børsen.

A similar examination of Danish foreign acquisitions was made by KonkurrenceRådet (1993), but this was limited to one year, 1992 . They used a similar approach, except that they screened a larger number of newspapers, etc., and their sample for 1992 included 85 acquisitions, of which 63.5% were made in either the U.K., Germany or the Scandinavian countries.[153] This distribution of countries is fairly consistent with that in Table 3.1, in which the same countries account for 60.9% of the sample in 1992. On the assumption that the sample from KonkurrenceRådet has included most of the acquisitions made in 1992 and that the sources used to collect the data in Table 3.1 have reported a constant ratio of the acquisitions actually made, it is estimated that approximately half of Danish foreign acquisitions made in the period 1988-1992 is included in the sample shown in Table 3.1.

[152] This bias is an advantage when the event study is conducted because it can be expected that the largest values of acquisitions made by companies listed on the Copenhagen Stock Exchange and their subsidiaries will be included in the sample.

[153] 14 acquisitions in the U.K., 14 acquisitions in Germany, and 26 acquisitions in the Scandinavian countries. See KonkurrenceRådet (1993), p. 39.

Moreover, Table 3.1 shows that Denmark's neighbours (U.K., Germany, Sweden and Norway), along with the U.S., account, by far, for the largest part of Danish foreign acquisitions in the period, namely 73%. This is consistent with Denmark's trade pattern: the largest proportion of exports is also channelled to Denmark's neighbours and the U.S. For the period 1988-1992, however, the fraction is only 53.7 % of total exports.[154]

To conduct the event study using stock market data, the initial sample had to be reduced until the remaining sample satisfied one of the following, additional criteria:

(3A) the acquiring company is to be listed on the Copenhagen Stock Exchange *or*
(3B) the acquiring company is to be a wholly-owned subsidiary of a company listed on the Copenhagen Stock Exchange.[155]

Applying criteria (3A) and (3B) left 107 acquisitions in the sample.

Central to event study methodology is the concept of *event days,* defined as the time relative to the announcement day. Here, time is defined as the number of trading days on the Copenhagen Stock Exchange, and the announcement day is defined as event day zero, where t=0. The announcement day of each acquisition is defined, for this study, as the date of the first acquisition announcement in *Børsen.*[156]

The event window, i.e., the period examined for abnormal returns, covers the period t = -5 days to t = +5 days. Because the data have to be »clean«[157] when analyzing the event window, yet another criterion has to be imposed on the sample:

(4) if the acquiring company made any other press releases about major corporate events[158] on different days in the period covered by the event window, then the acquisition must be excluded from the sample.

---

[154] Danmarks Statistik (the Danish office of statistics) (1994).

[155] Condition (3B) is imposed in order to exclude acquisitions expected only to have a limited effect on the stock price of the Danish mother company, e.g., when the acquisition is small and the subsidiary is only 51% owned. By far the largest consequence of condition (3B) is the exclusion of 15 acquisitions, made by Rentokil Group PLC, UK, from the sample.

[156] It is possible that the news of acquisitions reach the market the day preceding the event day, as press releases via the Copenhagen Stock Exchange are the most common way for acquiring companies to make the news public. The announcement and often also a »follow-up« story of the acquisition will thus appear the following day in *Børsen.* The date that the announcement appears in *Børsen* has been chosen as event date zero because it cannot be determined from the available sources whether the news reached the stock market before or after trading closed on the trading day prior to the announcement in *Børsen.*

[157] See the discussion of the clean data criterion in Chapter 3.1.1.

[158] For example, other acquisitions, annual accounts, new contracts and equity issues.

Note that companies with two or more acquisition announcements on the same event day are allowed in the sample because this will have no disturbing effect when calculating the daily *average* abnormal return.

As shown in Table 3.2, the reduced sample includes 92 foreign acquisitions. These acquisitions can be traced back to 40 different Danish parent companies.

Table 3.2: Frequency distribution of the reduced sample, by year and country

Country	1988		1989		1990		1991		1992		Total	
	No.	%	No.	%	No.	%	No.	%	No.	%	No.	%
U.K.	2	11	5	17	1	10	7	39	3	19	18	20
U.S.	8	44	4	13	2	20	3	17	1	6	18	20
Sweden	3	17	3	10	0	0	1	6	4	25	11	12
Germany	2	11	4	13	4	40	1	6	0	0	11	12
Norway	1	6	4	13	2	20	2	11	0	0	9	10
Netherlands	1	6	4	13	0	0	1	6	2	13	8	9
Others	1	6	6	20	1	10	3	17	6	38	17	18
Total	18	100	30	100	10	100	18	100	16	100	92	100
%	20	-	33	-	11	-	20	-	17	-	100	

Note: The procentages have been rounded off to the nearest integer.

Recall that information has to be new to the market as well as be economically relevant to the acquirer for the stock market to react with price changes. In the sample, five companies [159] separate themselves from the others by the number of foreign acquisitions they make.[160]

In an international context, these five companies follow what might be called a »growth by acquisition« strategy,[161] and because of this, the market might expect these companies to make a number of acquisitions along the same line on a continuous basis. Thus, acquisitions made by these companies will largely be

---

[159] These five companies are: S. Berendsen, Danisco, FLS, ISS and Superfos.

[160] In the five-year period studied, this group of companies made 46 acquisitions, equal to an average of 1.84 acquisitions per company per year, satisfying criteria (1) through (3B). Note that this number only includes acquisitions announced in *Børsen,* and it does *not* include the acquisitions made by Rentokil, S. Berendsen's UK subsidiary. The exclusion of Rentokil's acquisitions from the sample makes it less likely to accept the hypothesis that acquisitions by experienced acquirers are (partly) anticipated by the market when the lack of abnormal return on the event date might as well be due to the limited effect the acquisition would have on the Danish parent company.

[161] Note that all five companies explicitly mentioned acquisitions as a strategy in their annual reports.

anticipated by the stock market, implying that the stock market can only be expected to react with minor price adjustments (i.e., small $\overline{AR}_t$) to these companies' announcements of acquisitions.

To test if the stock market actually reacts as described above, the sample shown in Table 3.2 is divided into two subsamples: one subsample consisting of the acquisitions made by the five companies, labelled »major acquirers«, and another subsample consisting of all remaining acquisitions, labelled »other acquirers«. Table 3.3 shows the numbers of acquisitions included in the two subsamples.

Table 3.3: Frequency distribution of the reduced sample, by subsample and year

Subsample	1988	1989	1990	1991	1992	Total
	---------------number of acquisitions---------------					
Major Acquirers	6	8	3	7	6	30
Other Acquirers	12	21	7	12	10	62
Total	18	29	10	19	16	92

As mentioned in Chapter 3.1.1, the ownership structure of many Danish companies is special, making it possible for a relatively small group of owners to control the company. With respect to the Danish stock market, three types of company ownership are normal:

1. *family ownership,* where a person or a family controls a majority of the votes,
2. *foundation ownership,* where a foundation controls a majority of the votes, and
3. *diversified ownership,* where the company has several owners, and no single owner controls a majority of the votes.[162]

To analyze the dependence of the stock market reaction on ownership type of the acquiring company, the sample shown in Table 3.2 has been divided into three subsamples, each representing a specific type of ownership. This division is presented in Table 3.4.

Table 3.4: Frequency distribution of the reduced sample, by type of ownership

Type of Ownership	Family Ownership	Foundation Ownership	Diversified Ownership	Foreign Ownership*	Total
Number of acquisitions	24	16	46	6	92

*: a foreign company controls the voting majority

Sources: Strandskov, Thomsen & Pedersen (1994) and Greens (1992).

[162] The definitions used are similar to those used by Strandskov, Thomsen & Pedersen (1994).

In summary, this subsection has reported the construction of a data set containing the population of Danish foreign acquisitions made during the period 1988-1992. This has been established despite the lack of public, periodic statistics on the subject. To conduct an event study on the data, it has been necessary to impose a number of restrictions on the population to get a sample appropriate for the event study. The reduced sample consists of approximately 40% of the initially identified population and includes 92 acquisitions, which can be traced back to 40 different Danish parent companies.

2.3. Empirical Results of the Event Study

This subsection presents the results of the event study conducted on the data shown in Tables 3.3 and 3.4, using the definitions and test statistics developed in Chapter 3.1.2.

In conducting the event study, the number of acquisitions for which results actually can be calculated was reduced, due, in part, to infrequent trading of a large proportion of stocks quoted on the Copenhagen Stock Exchange.

An initial step in calculating the $AR_{j,t}$'s included running a regression on the $R_{j,t}$'s in the estimation period to get the parameter estimates (alpha and beta). To get sensible parameter estimates, an additional criterion was imposed on the sample, namely, that security *j* had to be traded on at least 80 of the 120 days in the estimation period.[163] Furthermore, in order to calculate the $AR_{j,t}$, security *j* had to be traded on each of the days included in the event window *and* on the day immediately before the event window began;[164] e.g., in event window t = [-5;5], security j had to be traded on each of the days *t* = [-6;5]. As previously mentioned, these additional practical criteria significantly reduced the number of acquisitions for which results actually can be calculated. As can be observed by comparing Tables 3.3 and 3.5, this reduction has occured almost entirely in the subsample »other acquirers«.

---

[163] The actual number of days with trades in the estimation period were by far greater than 80, for most of the observations for which *AR*'s were calculated. Additionally, very few of the excluded observations traded more than 50 days during the estimation period. Note: this criterion is referred to as criterion (5).

[164] The security also has to be traded on the day before the event windows started to avoid a possible significant result on day *t* = -5 caused by lagged price adjustment which itself would be due to a previous period without trade. Note: this criterion is referred to as criterion (6).

Table 3.5: $\overline{AR}_t$, t_t-values, and positive/negative $\overline{AR}_t$ ratios, by event days and subsample

Event day, t	Major Acquirers (N = 27)			Other Acquirers (N = 15)			All Acquirers (N = 42)		
	$\overline{AR}_t$ in %	t-value	positive : negative	$\overline{AR}_t$ in %	t-value	positive : negative	$\overline{AR}_t$ in %	t-value	positive : negative
-5	-0.24	-1.07	15:12	0.05	0.14	7:8	-0.14	-0.69	22:20
-4	-0.04	-0.18	14:13	0.16	0.42	9:6	0.03	0.15	23:19
-3	0.29	1.26	12:15	0,54	1.43	8:7	0.38	1.90°°	20:22
-2	-0.24	-1.08	10:17°	-0.06	-0.16	6:9	-0.18	-0.90	16:26°°
-1	0.18	0.80	16:11	-0.06	-0.15	6:9	0.10	0.49	22:20
0	-0.32	-1.41°	11:16	0.08	0.21	6:9	-0.18	-0.90	17:25°
1	-0.18	-0.80	10:17°	0.50	1.32	8:7	0.06	0.03	18:24
2	0.11	0.50	16:11	0.66	1.75°	10:5°	0.31	1.55°°	26:16°°
3	0.21	0.92	20:7**	-0.08	-0.20	6:9	0.10	0.53	26:16°°
4	-0.10	-0.42	12:15	0.90	2.39*	11:4*	0.26	1.31°°	23:19
5	-0.23	-1.00	14:13	0.16	0.42	7:8	-0.09	-0.45	21:21

° , °° , * , **: The null hypothesis of $\overline{AR}_t$, equal to zero, is rejected at the 90%, 95%, 97.5% or 99% - or better - level of confidence (one tailed test).

Table 3.5 shows the $\overline{AR}_t$ for the two subsamples and the total sample, respectively, along with the test statistic t_t and the binomial sign test on each of the days in an event window, beginning on day t=-5 and ending on day t=5.[165]

As is evident from Table 3.5, the Danish stock market reacts differently to acquisition announcements made by the two subsamples of companies. The stock market reacts quickly and negatively on acquisition announcements made by »major acquirers«, as these announcements are associated with negative and significant $\overline{AR}_t$ on the event days t=[0,1]. The stock market's reaction to acquisition announcements made by »other acquirers« is slightly lagged, but positive, as the $\overline{AR}_t$ are positive and (partly) significant on the event days t=[1,2,4].

---

[165] To take into account possible shifts in $\hat{\beta}_j$ (i.e., the security's market risk) due to the acquisition, results were also obtained by estimating the market model's parameters when using a pre- and post-acquisition estimation period. These results are presented in Appendix A. The signs as well as the sizes of the $\overline{AR}_t$ in Appendix A are consistent with the $\overline{AR}_t$ show in Table 3.5, although the significance of the t_t-values and the binomial sign tests vary slightly, as the t_t-values *outside* the period t=[-2;1] and the binomial sign tests *within* the period t=[-1;1] are both relatively more significant for the $\overline{AR}_t$ in Appendix A than the $\overline{AR}_t$ in Table 3.5.

The lagged reaction recorded for the subsample »other acquirers« could possibly result from a lower frequency of acquisitions made by this subsample than by »major acquirers«, thus implying that market participants take a longer time to evaluate an unfamiliar event than a familiar one. Similarly, the significant numbers of positive $AR_{j,t=3}$ for »major acquirers« may be price-adjusted to the negative reactions on the event days t=[0,1] after the market has had some time to further analyze the expected effects of the event on shareholder value. The number of positive $AR_{j,t=3}$ were highly significant, but because the price adjustments were relatively small, the size of the $\overline{AR}_t$ were not significant.

With respect to the total sample, the $\overline{AR}_t$ were not significant in the period t= [-1;1] as the $\overline{AR}_t$ of the two subsamples evened each other out. Outside this period, the results that were significant for one of the subsamples also caused significant results in the total sample.

The daily mean difference between the two subsamples, »major acquirers« and »other acquirers«, and their respective t-values are shown in Table 3.6.

Table 3.6: The daily mean difference of average abnormal returns (DAR) between » major acquirers« and » other acquirers« for the event window, t = [-5;5]

Event day, t	Daily Mean Difference (between »major acquirers« and »other acquirers«)	
	DAR i %	t-value
-5	-0.29	-0.71
-4	-0.20	-0.48
-3	-0.25	-0.61
-2	-0.19	-0.45
-1	-0.24	0.58
0	-0.40	-0.96
1	-0.68	-1.65°
2	-0.55	-1.32°
3	0.29	0.70
4	-1.00	-2.41*
5	-0.38	0.93

°, * : The null hypothesis, that $\overline{AR}_t$ (»major acquirers«) = $\overline{AR}_t$ (»other acquirers«), i.s., rejected at a 90% or 97.5% or better levels of confidence, respectively (one tailed test).

It is evident from Table 3.6 that, on event days t=[1,2,4], the $\overline{AR}_t$ of »other acquirers« were significantly different - more positive - from the $\overline{AR}_t$ of »major acquirers«. Moreover, from Table 3.6, it is quite evident that the stock market responded relatively more, in terms of the size of the $\overline{AR}_t$, and also relatively more favorably, to announcements made by »other acquirers« than »major acquirers«. The first effect - more response to acquisition announcements of »other acquirers« - is consistent with the assumption that the stock market had partly anticipated the acquisitions made by the subsample »major acquirers«[166] and, thus, partly incorporated the news into the prices.

Table 3.7 shows the cumulative abnormal return for different subsamples for the event day t=[-1,0], i.e., the day prior to the the acquisition announcement in *Børsen* and on the day of that announcement, and for the event day t=[-5;5].

Table 3.7: Cumulative abnormal return (CAR), on CAR-periods and subsamples

CAR-period	Major Acquirers (N=27)[a]		Other Acquirers (N=15)[a]		All Acquirers (N=42)[a]		Extended Sample (N=52)[b]	
	CAR in %	*Q*-value	*CAR* in %	*Q*-value	*CAR* in %	*Q*-value	*CAR* in %	*Q*-value
t = [-1;0]	-0.14	-0.43	0.02	0.01	-0.08	-0.29	0.14	0.55
t = [-5;5]	-0.56	-1.76°°	2.85	5.34**	0.66	2.34*		

a: security j was traded on each of the days in the period t=[-6;5].
b: security j was traded on each of the days in the period t=[-2;0].
°°, *, **: The null hypothesis, that *CAR* is equal to zero, is rejected at a 95%, 97.5% or 99% or better level of confidence (one tailed test).

Again, it is evident that the stock market reacted more positively to acquisition announcements made by »other acquirers« than those made by »major acquirers«. This is especially evident with respect to the 11-day event window, where the $CAR_{[-5;5]}$ is significantly negative for »major acquirers« and significantly positive for »other acquirers«. It has been possible to extend the *CAR* analysis with the event window t=[-1;0], and the »extended sample« includes the observations where security j was traded on each of the days t=[-2,-1,0].[167] All of the additional observations in the »extended sample« fall into the category »other acquirers«, and it is evident that the stock market's reaction to these additional observations are very positive, even if none of the Q-values in Table 3.7 are significant.

The »extended sample« has also been analyzed for the importance of ownership structure to the determination of the $\overline{AR}_t$. Table 3.8 shows the $\overline{AR}_t$, their respective t-values and binomial sign tests for the three ownership types on the event days t=[-1,0].

[166] The subsample »major acquirers« consisted of companies which followed a »growth by acquisition strategy« and conducted acquisitions on a regular basis.

[167] See criterion (6).

Table 3.8: The $\overline{AR}_t$, t-values and positive/negative $\overline{AR}_t$ ratios, by event days and acquirer's ownership type

Event day	Acquirers with Diversified Ownership (N = 32)			Foundation-owned Acquirers (N = 9)			Family-owned Acquirers (N = 11)		
	$\overline{AR}_t$ in %	t-value	positive : negative	$\overline{AR}_t$ in %	t-value	positive : negative	$\overline{AR}_t$ in %	t-value	positive : negative
-1	0.17	0.81	16 : 16	0.67	1.62*	4 : 5	-0.17	-0.36	6 : 5
0	-0.09	-0.42	17 : 15	-0.14	-0.33	3 : 6*	0.15	0.32	5 : 6

* : The null hypothesis, that $\overline{AR}_t$ is equal to zero, is rejected at a 90% or better level of confidence (one tailed test).

It is evident from Table 3.8 that the stock market responded most positively to acquisition announcements made by foundation-owned acquirers. The $\overline{AR}_{t=-1}$ for the subsample »foundation-owned acquirers« are positive and the only significant $\overline{AR}_t$ in Table 3.8. The binomial sign test shows that there is a very even distribution between positive and negative $\overline{AR}_t$ in the three subsamples, except for foundation-owned acquirers on event day t=−1.

In Table 3.9, the daily mean difference between the three subsamples representing the three types of ownership and their respective D-values are shown.

Table 3.9: Daily mean difference of the average abnormal return (DAR) between different ownership types for event days t=[-1,0]

Event day	Daily Mean Difference					
	»Acquirers with Diversified Ownership« minus »Foundation-owned Acquirers«		»Foundation-owned Acquirers« minus »Family-owned Acquirers«		»Acquirers with Diversified Ownership« minus »Family-owned Acquirers«	
	DAR in %	*D*-value	DAR in %	*D*-value	DAR in %	*D*-value
1	-0.50	-1.10	0.84	1.31	0.34	0.76
0	0.05	0.10	-0.29	-0.45	-0.24	-0.53

Although none of the D-values in Table 3.9 were significant, it seems like the stock market response is most favorable to acquisition announcements made by foundation-owned acquirers.

Because event study methodology focuses only on fully diversified investors,[168] the results shown in Tables 3.8 and 3.9 could be interpreted to mean that the interests of fully diversified investors are best served by acquisitions made by foundation owned companies. However, caution should be taken in drawing strong conclusions based on Tables 3.8 and 3.9, due to the small sample size and the insignificance of most of the results.

To summarize this subsection, the stock market reacts more quickly, but less positively, to acquisition announcements coming from »major acquirers« as opposed to »other acquirers«. These results confirm that the segmentation of the total sample into subsamples representing different acquisition frequencies was warranted.

The $CAR_{t=[-1;0]}$ was not statistically significant, neither for the total sample (»all acquirers«) nor for the subsamples representing different acquisition frequencies. However, the $CAR_{t=[-5;5]}$ was statistically significant and positive for »other acquirers« as well as for the total sample. This thus leads to a rejection of hypothesis H1 for these subsamples. It is, however, not possible to reject hypothesis H1 for the subsample labelled »major acquirers« because the $CAR_{t=[-5;5]}$, was both negative and statistically significant. This indicates some support for the predictions of Roll's »hubris hypothesis«[169] with respect to »major acquirers«, even if it is somewhat of a paradox that experienced acquirers should suffer from hubris![170]

With respect to hypothesis H2, it was only on event days t=[1,2,4] that the DAR's are significantly different for the subsamples »major acquirers« and »other acquirers«.

The $CAR_{t=[-1,0]}$ of the total sample was not significantly different from zero, nor is the »extended sample«, even if the $CAR_{t=[-1,0]}$ of the »extended sample« is positive, in contrast to »all acquirers«. When the »extended sample« was divided into three subsamples, each representing a type of ownership, the foundation-owned acquirers was the only subsample with an $\overline{AR}_t$ significantly different from zero. It was also positive. Thus hypothesis H1 was rejected for acquirers with foundation ownship and inconclusive for the other subsamples. It was not possible to find any statistically significant difference in the changes of shareholder value among any of the subsamples representing different ownership types. Thus hypothesis H2 was rejected for these subsamples.

---

168 See Chapter 2. Because most of the A-shares are most commonly held by the controlling family or foundation and thus are not for sale, it is not possible to use the event study method to analyze the expected effect on shareholder value to this group of owners.

169 See Chapter 2.3.2. The »hubris hypothesis« predicts a price decline on announcement of a bid with respect to the bidding firm, i.e., the acquirer.

170 It is not possible to make any conclusions with respect to Jensen's »free cash flow hypothesis« on the sample tested because the data was not suitable for this. See Chapter 3.2.1.

3. The Second Test: Validity of the Danish Stock Market's Appraisal of Danish International Acquisitions 1988-1992

In this section, the market efficiency research programme's assumption of an unbiased price reaction to new information is tested. As the market efficiency research programme focuses on shareholder value, a viable method for testing the unbiasedness assumption would be to compare the long term development in shareholder value of a portfolio of acquiring companies to a compatible portfolio of non-acquiring companies. In this way, it would be possible to explore the long term effects of acquisitions and to see if acquirers are able to realize pursued acquisition gains in terms of shareholder value. It is, however, not possible to employ this method with the data used in Chapter 3.2 because it is impossible to create a portfolio compatible with a portfolio of the acquiring companies.[171] An alternative method for testing the unbiasedness assumption would be to compare the stock market's reaction with the actual acquisition results as they are perceived by the management of the acquiring company. This method is not ideal since actual acquisition results are not necessarily correlated with the development in shareholder value. However, the method has the advantage of taking the actual acquisition results into account and hereby addressing the critique often raised by scholars of strategy, namely that stock market measures are not necessarily a good measure of actual acquisition results.

Chapter 3.3.1 introduces the applied method in further detail and presents the additional data needed to conduct the test. Chapter 3.3.2 presents the results of the test.

3.1. The Applied Method and the Additional Data

Comparison of the stock market's reaction to management's assessment of actual acquisition results is done by plotting the $CAR_{[-5;5]}$ against an index expressing management's assessment of the actual acquisition results. Two plots are conducted. In the first plot, the index measures management's assessment of the development in the target's economic results since the time of the acquisition. This measure (labelled »economic result«) has been chosen because one may expect a connection between a positive development in the economic result and a positive development in shareholder value.

In the second plot, the index measures management's assessment of the development in the target's business opportunities since the time of the acquisition. This measure (labelled »business opportunities«) has been chosen mainly because it is important to know if the acquisition is motivated by strategic reasons, but also because favorable business opportunities are expected to be important for positive development in a company's future economic result - and subsequently also in its shareholder value.

---

171 For example, it is not possible to find two companies compatible with ISS and Sophus Berendsen on the Copenhagen Stock Exchange that are not engaging in acquisition activities.

The plots will make it possible to visually examine the correlation between the $CAR_{[-5;5]}$ and the respective measures. As a supplement to the plots, a calculation is made of the statistical correlations between the $CAR_{[-5;5]}$ and each of the measures.

In the tests, i.e., the plots and the statistical correlation, the following hypothesis is tested:

H3: *There is a positive correlation between the $CAR_{[-5;5]}$-values and the index-values of the respective measures, i.e., »economic result« and »business opportunities«.*

If H3 is accepted, then the $CAR_{[-5;5]}$-values are good indicators of the acquiring companies' managements' assessment of actual acquisition results with respect to the targets' economic result and business opportunities. If H3 is rejected, however, this could reflect one of the following causes:

- the stock market's predictions - embedded in the $CAR_{[-5;5]}$-values - are *not* unbiased (it is here implicitly assumed that »economic result« and »business opportunities« are good indicators of future shareholder value) or
- the stock market's predictions - embedded in the $CAR_{[-5;5]}$-values - *are* unbiased (it is here implicitly assumed that »economic result« and »business opportunities« are poor indicators of future shareholder value).

To obtain the additional, needed data for the measures »economic result« and »business opportunities« for this second test, a questionnaire was constructed.[172] One questionnaire per acquisition was send to the companies conducting the 42 acquisitions tested in Chapter 3.2.3.[173] After two reminders,[174] a response rate of 50%, i.e., 21 questionnaires, were obtained, although only 20 of the questionnaires were usable for this test. The data collected for the two measures are shown in Table 3.10.

---

[172] The questionnaire was also used to explore some factual data about the target companies (data which was not obtainable otherwise) and data about the acquirers' actual acquisition appraisal. This data is presented in Chapter 5.2.

[173] See »all acquirers« in Table 3.5.

[174] Before the questionnaire was sent out, the company was contacted by phone to introduce the study and to inform the respondents of the questionnaire. About 14 days after the respondents received the questionnaire, another contact - a reminder - was made by phone to those respondents which had not answered already. Finally, after another 14 days, a follow-up letter was sent to the respondents which still had not answered the questionnaire.

Table 3.10: Data used for the plots

		Index 1: disagree very much				5: agree very much	Total	$CAR_{[-5;5]}$
		1	2	3	4	5		
		number of answers						%
Statement to be indexed by management in the questionnaire	The target's economic result is better today than expected at the time of the acquisition	2	2	5	3	8	20	0.7799
	The target's business opportunities have developed more positively than expected at the time of the acquisition	3	1	8	7	1	20	0.7799
Acquirers which did not answer the questionnaire *		N.A.	N.A.	N.A.	N.A.	N.A.	22	0,5510

*: includes one questionnaire that did not answer the two statements.
N.A.: not available

3.2. Empirical Results of the Test

This subsection presents the results from the examination of the comparison of the stock market's reaction to management's assessment of actual acquisition results. The data used is presented in Table 3.10, along with the individual $CAR_{[-5;5]}$-values.[175] Figure 3.1 presents the first plot.

[175] These values were previously calculated to produce the data for Table 3.7. See Chapter 3.2.3.

Figure 3.1: Plot of $CAR_{[-5;5]}$-values against the index-values

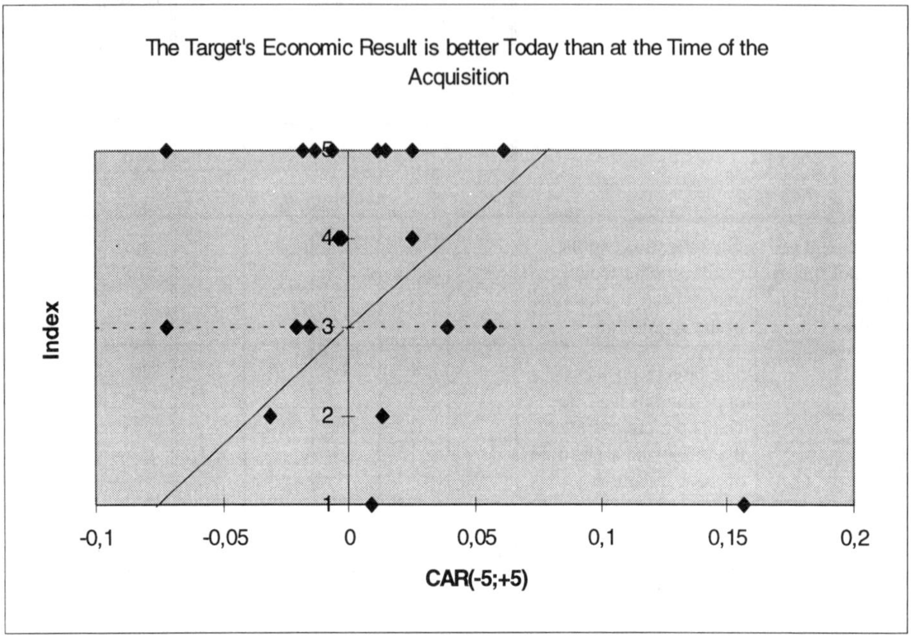

In the following, it is assumed that the acquisition is a borderline investment in the acquiring company's appraisal, i.e., that is, net present value is just on the positive side of zero.[176] By making this additional assumption, the index-value »3«, i.e., neither agree nor disagree, is made equal to the $CAR_{[-5;5]}$-value »0«. The plot is divided into four quadrants by letting the dotted line (index-value=3) cross the y-axis ($CAR_{[-5;5]}$-value=0). An acceptance of hypothesis H3 requires that coordinates are located in the upper right quadrant or the lower left quadrant. The line passing through these squares illustrates one possible line around which the coordinates would be located if correlation between the $CAR_{[-5;5]}$-values and the index-values were positive.[177]

If the coordinates are located in either the upper left quadrant or the lower right quadrant, they indicate an incorrect appraisel by the stock market of the acquisitions. Coordinates in the upper left quadrante indicate acquisitions the stock market has appraised too negatively and coordinates in the lower right quadrant indicate acquisitions that the stock market has appraised too positively.

If the coordinates located on the lines shaping the four quadrants are discarded, then there are slightly more »too negative« appraisals that »too positive appraisals« (5 as opposed to 3). Furthermore, it is evident that when the stock market's appraisal

[176] See Chapter 4.1 for further details about the net present value principle.

[177] The line's slope will vary according to how positive the correlation is.

is positive, then the $CAR_{[-5;5]}$-values are more likely to be positively correlated with the index-values than if the stock market's appraisal is negative. The number of coordinates in the upper left quadrant and the lower right quadrant are slightly higher than the number of coordinates in the upper right quadrant and the lower left quadrant, thus indicating a rejection of hypothesis H3 (8 as opposed to 6). This rejection is confirmed by the calculated statistical correlation between the $CAR_{[-5;5]}$-values and the index values; it is slightly negative (-0.29992).[178]

However, it not possible to reject the unbiasedness hypothesis on this basis and especially not when the $CAR_{[-5;5]}$-values for the acquirers not answering the questionnaire are taken into account (see Table 3.10). The non-answering acquirers' $CAR_{[-5;5]}$-values are lower than the $CAR_{[-5;5]}$-values of the acquirers answering the questionnaire, and this leads to the suspicion that the non-answering acquirers have experienced less positive acquisition results than expected, i.e., an indication of a correct stock market appraisal.

Figure 3.2: Plot of $CAR_{[-5;5]}$-values against the index-values

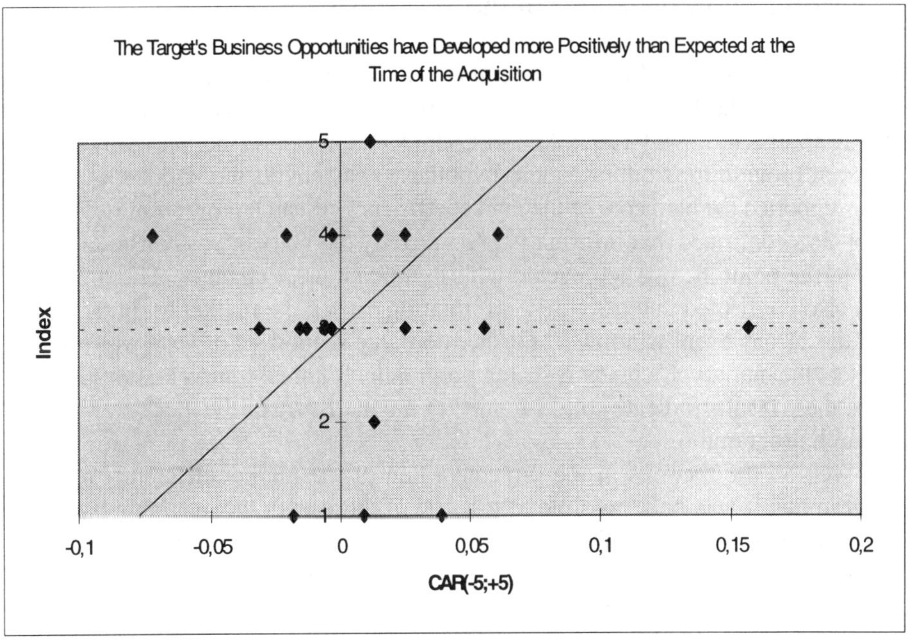

The second plot is shown in Figure 3.2. Again, the same pattern as in Figure 3.1 is evident. When the stock market's appraisal is positive, then the $CAR_{[-5;5]}$-values are more likely to be positively correlated with the index-values than when the stock

[178] And the $R^2 = 0.08995$.

market's appraisal is negative.[179] Furthermore, the number of coordinates in the upper left quadrant and the lower right quadrant are slightly higher than the number of coordinates in the upper right quadrant and the lower left quadrant, again indicating a rejection of hypothesis H3 (6 as opposed to 5). Once again, this rejection is supported by the calculated statistical correlation, which also is slightly negative (-0.12541).[180] However the number of coordinates in the upper left quadrant is identical to the number of coordinates in the lower right quadrant, i.e., the stock market appraisals are as much on the negative side as on the positive side, in terms of frequency.

On the basis of the tests conducted in this section, the conclusion of the test of the validity of the market efficiency research programme's unbiasedness hypothesis is that it has not been possible to reject the hypothesis that the Danish stock markets' reaction with respect to the appraisal of foreign acquisitions in the period 1988-1992 was unbiased.

4. Theoretical Implications of the Two Tests

In Chapter 3, two set of tests were conducted. In Chapter 3.2, an event study was conducted of the Danish stock market's appraisal of Danish foreign acquisitions during the period 1988-1992. And in Chapter 3.3, a test of the market efficiency research programme's unbiasedness hypothesis was conducted. Both sets of tests have supported the hard core of the market efficiency research programme. The first set of tests confirmed that information received by the market was considered truly new to the point the market reacted with significant price changes. The first set of tests also confirmed that truly new information caused the market to, in fact, react over the 11-day event window.[181] Furthermore, the second set of tests was not able to reject the market efficiency research programme's unbiasedness assumption. All in all, these results indicate solid support for the hard core of the market efficiency research programme.

Given all the theories in the protective belt of the market efficiency research programme, it was only possible to test one of these with the available data. The theory tested was Roll's »hubris hypothesis«. The »hubris hypothesis« was rejected for the overall sample consisting of Danish foreign acquisitions in the period 1988-1992.[182] However, when the overall sample was divided into two subsamples representing different acquisition frequencies, then the »hubris hypothesis« was supported by the subsample representing the most frequent acquirers, i.e., »major

---

179 There are 4 coordinates in the upper right square as opposed to 1 coordinate in the lower left square.

180 And the $R^2 = 0.01572$.

181 See the $CAR_{[-5;+5]}$-analysis.

182 See the $CAR_{[-5;+5]}$-analysis.

acquirers«, and not supported by the subsample representing the less frequent acquirers, i.e., »other acquirers«. These results are somewhat paradoxical given Roll's suggestion, in the context of the »hubris hypothesis«, that the reason for acquirers' over-estimation of acquisition gains is the lack of recurring acquisition decisions in the managers' careers!

Unfortunately, it was not possible to test if Jensen's »free cash flow hypothesis« provided a better explanation for the sample of Danish foreign acquisitions in the period 1988-1992 than Roll's »hubris hypothesis«. This was because Danish legislation affects the data needed for the test. The literature accounted for in Chapters 3.2.1 and 3.2.2 was, however, more supportive of Jensen's »free cash flow hypothesis« than Roll's »hubris hypothesis«.

PART 2

Acquisition Appraisal - The Acquiring Company's Perspective

The financial literature on acquisitions has mostly been concerned with appraising if acquisitions were good investments from a stock market perspective. This issue was addressed in Part 1 of this book using an investigation of the Danish stock market's appraisal of Danish foreign acquisitions over the period 1988-1992. Within the financial literature on acquisitions, little attention has been given to whether the conclusions drawn with respect to the stock market[183] are also valid from a company perspective, and if so, what the acquiring companies could do to improve their appraisal of the companies they considered acquiring. In Part 1, an examination was made of the applicability of the stock market's reaction to the company perspective, and the conclusion drawn was that it was not possible to reject the hypothesis that the stock market's reaction is unbiased with respect to the acquiring managers' assessment of the acquisition's success. Because the stock market had a negative reaction to some acquisitions this conclusion implies that greater emphasis is needed on how the appraisal of acquisitions can be improved on the company level.

This part of the book will deal with this exact issue. In doing so, it follows Popper's schema of the scientific process,[184] however, not from the same starting point as in Part 1. First, the problem is illuminated and explored. Because the problem, of how acquisition appraisal on a company level can be improved, is a theoretical as well as a practical one, it will be addressed both theoretically and practically. With respect to the theoretical part of the problem, Lakatos' MSRP will also be used here as an explanatory framework. Second, a solution to the problem, i.e., a tentative theory, is presented.

To address problems of how acquisition appraisal on the company level can be improved, an identification will be made of financial theories that can be utilized and operationalized for company appraisal. This is done in Chapter 4, using Lakatos' MSRP as an explanatory framework. The net present value (NPV) principle

[183] Recall that the conclusion generally drawn in these empirical studies is that, on average, acquisitions do not appear to produce a gain to stockholders in the acquiring company.

[184] See footnote 22.

constitutes the hard core of the research programme. The protective belt of the research programme consists of methods operationalizing the NVP principle as well as theories extending the applicability of the hard core. Quite interestingly, all the theories belonging to the research programme are logical theories. This implies it is not possible to falsify these theories empirically and thus use empirical falsification as a means for addressing the theoretical part of the problem.

It is, however, possible to examine empirically how logical theories are operationalized and what problems arise in the process. This is one of the issues addressed in Chapter 5, which explores actual acquisition appraisal of acquiring companies in order to uncover some of the aspects that could lead to an improvement of acquisition appraisal on a company level.

In Chapter 6, the theoretical framework from Chapter 4 is integrated into the resource-coherency theory. It is shown, on the basis of examples from Chapter 5, how this integrated framework enables a company to improve its acquisition appraisal so that, by applying a single approach in its acquisition appraisal, it will achieve both a strategic and a monetary appraisal of the target company.

CHAPTER 4

The Net Present Value (NPV) Research Programme

This chapter will present what has been named the net present value (NPV) research programme. The NPV research programme is dominated by logical theories,[185] both in the hard core of the research programme and in its protective belt. In this respect, the NPV research programme differs from the market efficiency research programme presented in Part 1 and from most other research programmes by not including empirical theories in its protective belt.

The hard core of the NPV research programme is the NPV principle, and it is presented in the first section of this chapter. In the same section, two other logical models are presented. These represent two theories that are variations of the NPV principle. In the second section of this chapter, the negative and positive heuristics of the research programme are presented. No anomalies are presented in this section because anomalies do not exist in a logical research programme if the research programme is consistent with itself.

The research programme's protective belt is presented in the third section of this chapter. First, this section presents some of the methods used to operationalize the NPV principle, and second, it explains how the NPV principle can be extended using option theory. In the final section of this chapter, the NPV research programme is assessed using Lakatos' MSRP framework.

1. The Hard Core: The NPV Principle

The theories presented in this section all contain a common feature, namely the calculatation of the present value (PV) of money given the future value (FV) of money. In the following review of these theories, focus will be on the net values[186]

---

[185] According to H.Nørreklit (1993): logical theories are theories »... based on rational reasoning without empirical postulates about the human behavior that their uses depend on.« p. 1; author's translation. See also Chapter 1.3.1.

[186] The net PV = positive PV - negative PV ; and the net FV = positive FV - negative FV.

primarily to keep the formula simple,[187] but also because the assessment of net values, rather than gross values, is important to the investment decision. The NPV principle is defined mathematically as follows:

$$(9) \quad NPV = \sum_{t=0}^{T} NFV_t \cdot \frac{1}{(1+r)^t}$$

where:

NPV: net present value
NFV_t: net future value i.e. net cash flow; at time t [188]
r: the discount rate
T: the time horizon

Within the literature, the NPV principle is considered superior for evaluating and ranking investment proposals. One of the advantages of the NPV principle is the value additivity principle (VAP), i.e., that it is possible to add present values together because they are all measured at the same point in time. The important implications of the VAP can best be illustrated by an example. Assume that, within a specific company, 10 different and mutually independent processes are carried out. Each of these processes generates and/or uses cash flow on a continuing basis. For each of these processes, the NPV can be calculated. And due to the VAP, it is also possible to calculate the NPV of the company as a whole: it is just the sum of the NPV's of the 10 processes. The VAP should, however, be treated with some care as it is vital to the VAP that the projects (or processes) added together are truly independent, i.e., none of the project's cash flows is affected by the operation or non-operation of any of the other projects. If two projects affect each other's cash flow when employed together, then their combined NPV, i.e., NPV (project 1 + project 2), has to be calculated before the VAP can be used.

When the NPV principle is employed, then the decision rule to undertake a new investment (or to continue with an old one) is quite simple:

undertake (or continue) the investment if its NPV>0

or if there are several mutually exclusive investments to choose among:

choose the investment(s) which maximizes the NPV

As mentioned previously, the NPV principle is a logical theory, but it is also the logical theory constituting the basis for two other logical theories on this subject, namely, the discounted payback (DPB) model and the internal rate of return (IRR) model. Similar to the NPV principle, both models uses formula (9) in their

---

[187] For the same reason, taxes and inflation will be disregarded.

[188] The initial cash flow (often a cost) is incorporated into the formula when t=0.

calculations;[189] but contrary to the NPV principle, they do not focus on the NPV, rather they focus on T and r, respectively.

The DPB model calculates how many periods, i.e., the critical value of T *(payback period)*, a project operates before the NPV equals zero (or is just slightly positive),[190] and the IRR model calculates the discount rate, i.e., internal rate of return *(irr)*, at which a project's NPV equals zero.[191]

Compared to the NPV principle, however, both models have shortcomings. The DPB model ignores the cash flow, i.e., NFV in formula (9), which falls after the cut-off date, i.e., the *payback period*. This becomes a problem when choosing among several projects if one or more of the projects generates cash flow after the cut-off date. This can result in an NPV that is not maximized. Although the DPB model is not well regarded among scholars due to its ad hoc nature, it is very popular and much used among practitioners.

The IRR model has several shortcomings, according to Brealy & Myers (1988):[192]

1. the IRR model does not indicate whether the *irr* accrues from positive or negative cash flows, i.e., due to borrowing or lending, because it is positive in both cases;
2. if there is more than one change of sign in the cash flows, then the *irr* will not be unique;
3. choosing the project with the highest *irr* is not necessarily the same as maximizing the NPV; if the total inflow of a project compared to another is larger, but occurs later, then it will have the lowest *irr*, but the highest NPV;
4. the IRR model cannot cope with interest rates that vary over time; while the *irr* is a constant, the opportunity cost of capital can vary over time.

Although the IRR model has more shortcomings than the DPB model, it is still preferred to the DPB model by finance scholars, mainly because the latter is too ad hoc in nature.

To summarize: the NPV principle - which comprises the hard core of the research programme presented in this chapter - is considered *the* correct method for investment appraisal by scholars. It is also preferred over both the DPB and IRR models because it overcomes the shortcomings of these two models.[193] The hard

---

[189] Because the DPB and IRR models originate from formula (9), as the NPV principle does, they will be presented in this section and not in the third section of this chapter. This is further motivated by the fact that neither the DPB nor the IRR model makes any empirical assumptions. The only additional assumption made in these two cases is that the NPV = 0.

[190] The DPB model can also be calculated so that T, the pay back period, must equal a specific number of years. The DPB model would then check to see if the NPV$\geq$0, and if the project therefore should be undertaken.

[191] This is the same as requiring that $r >$ the opportunity cost of capital.

[192] pp. 79-85.

[193] So far, only the logical implications of the models have been considered. Chapter 4.3 will deal with problems arising from operationalization of the models.

core of the NPV research programme can be reduced to the following two statements:

1. the NPV is calculated according to formula (9) and
2. an investment should be made in order to maximize the NPV.

2. The Negative and Positive Heuristics of the NPV Research Programme

The research programme presented in this chapter differs from the one presented in Chapter 2 in that it consists predominantly of logical theories. The hard core of the research programme is purely logical, and it is only via empirical assumptions made by the different methods or approaches within the protective belt that the hard core can be applied to the real world. As logical theories are true by definition,[194] the negative heuristic of the NPV research programme seems quite apparent:

Because the hard core is true, we should not hold it responsible for any problems in the application of the hard core, i.e., the NPV principle, to reality.

If there are problems in the application of the hard core to reality, then the positive heuristic of the research programme give us directions on how to deal with these problems. The positive heuristic of the NPV research programme can be stated as follows:

Any revision or modification of the research programme is done by changing or modifying the assumption(s) of a theory/method or the theory/method itself within the protective belt.

The NPV research programme differs from most other research programme in that it is not scholars, but rather practitioners who apply the hard core to reality. This difference is probably the main reason for the fairly slow development of the NPV research programme. Scholars have perhaps had a tendency to disregard the problems of operationalizing[195] the NPV principle in reality, believing that these problems arose as a result of practitioners' misuse of the NPV principle and their lack of theoretical knowledge, among other things. Subsequently, scholars - at least within the finance area - have not devoted much time to the development of this empirical aspect of the NPV research programme. Within more recent years, the main theoretical contribution to the development of the research programme has been the incorporation of option theories into the protective belt of the NPV research programme; these are also logical theories!

---

194 At least if they are consistent with themselves.

195 Donaldson (1984) discusses some of the conflicts between management's strategic investment choices and the NPV principle in an empirical study he undertook.

As a consequence of the tendency to disregard problems associated with operationalizing the NPV principle in reality (and not developing the theories in the protective belt), there has not been any real need for the positive heuristic or for further development of its guidelines. The negative heuristic has turned out to be quite sufficient.

3. The Protective Belt

The theories or methods belonging to the protective belt of the NPV research programme can be divided into two categories: those dealing with the operationalization of the NPV principle, i.e., its applicability to reality; and those extending the NPV principle. This section will deal with both categories.

3.1. Methods for Operationalizing the NPV Principle

This subsection will present the methods most commonly recommended by scholars for operationalizing the NPV principle. For this purpose, each of the elements in formula (9) will be dealt with in turn.

Before the NPV principle can be applied, it is essential to identify the type of investment to be evaluated, because different types of investments demand different types of input to formula (9). Assuming the NPV principle is to be applied to a specific company, then this investment could be seen either as an investment in shares or as an investment in real assets. These two types of investments demand different types of input to formula (9). However, when appraising a company as a whole, the two methods should, in principle, lead to the same result because it is generally assumed within finance that the market value of a company is equal to the sum of the values of all the company's individual projects.[196] For the sake of completeness, the input required for each investment type will be dealt with in the following.

The most important input to formula (9) is the future cash flow given the aim to compute the NPV of the future cash flow. In calculating the NPV of an investment, *all* future cash flows,[197] either generated from or affected by the investment, should be taken into account. Then the net FV (NFV), i.e., the future cash inflow less the future cash outflow, can be calculated for each period, and the NFV_t values are readily usable as input to formula (9).

In appraising a company as a *real asset*, the estimation of cash flows is normally based on the company's cash operating income,[198] i.e., a more aggregated cash flow estimate, and not on the cash flows accruing from its individual projects. This approach is also appropriate as long as all the effects of the investments in the

[196] In Chapter 6.1 this assumption will be questioned, but until then, it will be assumed to be valid.

[197] Sunk cost is not a future cash flow and hence should not be included in the calculation.

[198] That is, net income plus depreciation and other non-cash charges.

individual projects, including those arising from dependence between projects,[199] are taken into account in estimating future cash flows, i.e., the future cash operating income. If the appraisal, on the other hand, is based on the sum of the individual projects, more emphasis should be placed on establishing the correct boundaries between projects[200] and securing that all income or costs have been included, and included only once, in the estimates of the projects' NFV. Dependence between projects should, of course, still be taken into account.

When appraising a company on a *stock basis*, the NFV's consist of expected dividends for each of the years stock is held and the expected terminal value of the stock.[201] If acquisition of the stock is assumed to have an effect on expected dividends, then this should, of course, be taken into account, although it is normally not expected that a change in stock ownership would have such an effect. To obtain a change in expected dividends, it is expected that actual changes in the management of a company is necessary. This approach for appraising a target company is not recommended by scholars who believe in stock market's efficiency if there are no plans to change management of the company after the acquisition. That is because the correct NPV of the stock would then be the target company's current market price.[202]

After the NFV's have been identified, the next step is to find the correct discount rate, i.e., r in formula (9). Myers, as well as other scholars, considers the correct discount rate (r_s) to be:[203]

». . .the opportunity cost of capital, defined as the equilibrium expected rate of return on securities equivalent in risk to the project being valued.«

Because r_s is derived from the stock market, it would clearly be the correct discount rate to use when appraising a company on a *stock basis*. Whether r_s is the correct discount rate to use when appraising a company on a *real asset* basis can be - and is - discussed. If r_s is used, the discount rate is the same as that used by the owners

---

199 For example, an acquiring company planning to close an assembly line after the acquisition needs not only to take into account the direct changes in the company's cash operating income due to this when estimating the NFVs, but it also needs to take into account any additional effects, e.g., a higher overhead on the remaining activities, employees' re-education cost etc.

200 It is especially important, when appraising a potential acquisition candidate, if a project, e.g., an assembly line, has to be abandoned after the acquisition. If the NFV-boundaries between two projects are not correctly made, then this would form the basis for bad decisions.

201 In some calculations, it is assumed that stock is held indefinitely, and therefore, the expected terminal value should not be included in the formula.

202 See the discussion of the unbiasedness assumption of the market efficiency hypothesis in Chapter 2.

203 Myers (1984), p. 127.

of the acquiring company, i.e., the stockholders, and in principle,[204] the project is appraised to maximize the stockholders' NPV, i.e., the stock price. Many finance scholars favour this, as they view the main goal of a company as the maximization of shareholder value.[205] But is r_s necessarily equal to the opportunity cost of capital for a company with respect to a specific project? Well, it is possible that a large company may be able to obtain cheaper financing than its (smaller) competitors can, solely due to its size, i.e., importance to the lenders,[206] and hence its opportunity cost of capital for a specific project may be lower than the r_s.

Other scholars[207] however recommend that the acquiring company's weighted average cost of capital (r_c)[208] be used as the discount rate.[209] If the project is associated with the same risk as that of the company on average, then the use of r_c would be correct. On the other hand, if the project is associated with either a significantly higher or lower risk than that of the company on average, then the NPV would be biased higher or lower, respectively, than the correct NPV, i.e., towards a more or less likely acceptance of the project, respectively. As the previous

---

204 That is, if the company's estimates of NFV and the time horizon are the same as the stock market's.

205 See also Chapter 2.3.

206 For example, Hymer (1968):»The relative advantages of the market decreases as the firm is growing and profit from control and order is increasing. A striking example of the scale economies thus made possible is provided by loan operations. In order to check that a debitor is solvent and that the management of the firm is correct, the creditor needs many pieces of information. When a financial institution lends money to many small firms, each loan will be negotiated by a subordinate whose information and freedom of action will be limited. The amount of the loan will tend to be proportional to the amount of information available; small firms can usually borrow only very small amounts of money and only against secured collateral. A large firm, on the other hand, can provide more information and negotiate with the lender at a higher level of authority. The average cost of the operation is lower and the amount of money lent tends to be higher.«

207 See Weaver et al. (1991), p. 88.

208
$$r_c = r_d * (\frac{D}{E+D}) + r_e * (\frac{E}{D+E})$$

where

r_d = *cost of debt*
r_e = *cost of equity*
D = *debt*
E = *equity*

209 Note, if tax effects are disregarded. then $r_c = r_s$ calculated on the same company will be identical. However this does not imply that an r_s for an investment (e.g., a target company) will be equal to the acquirer's r_c.

discussion indicates, there are several aspects that need to be taken into account when r is estimated. However, Myers (1984) lends some consolation:[210]

»In my opinion, estimating cash flows properly is more important than fine-tuning the discount rate.«

If the cash flow and the discount rate(s)[211] are estimated for the expected lifetime of the project, as generally recommended by scholars, then the time horizon, T, is given. However, when the NPV principle is applied in reality, most companies use a standard time horizon, e.g., 5 or 10 years, for estimating NFV's and r. But when this approach is followed, these companies are in fact no longer using the NPV principle; rather, they are using the DPB model.[212] In this respect, it is important to realize that the demand for a higher return on the project increases as the time horizon is lowered.

The final aspect considered in this subsection of operationalizing the NPV principle is the treatment of foreign currency in an NPV analysis. Given a project, such as a foreign acquisition, the project's cash flow will then be denominated in another currency - the acquiring company's home currency. There are three methods which the acquiring company can use to appraise the project:[213]

1. the project can be appraised solely in the foreign currency, i.e., NFV's and the NPV can both be denominated in the foreign currency
2. the project can first be appraised in the foreign currency and afterwards the NPV can be translated back to the acquirer's home currency using the current currency rate, i.e., first NFV's and the NPV are denominated in the foreign currency, and then the NPV is translated into the home currency.
3. the NFV's can be converted into the home currency using the expected currency rates at time t and then the NPV can be calculated and the project appraised, i.e., NFV's and the NPV are both denominated in the home currency

If the expected currency rates at time t are assumed to be constant and equal to the current currency rate, then approaches 2 and 3 would give the same result. However, this assumption is quite restrictive, and hence the two approaches will most likely differ. Approach 2 is recommended if an appraisal in home currency is warranted, as this approach does not confuse the estimated value derived from the real investment with value derived from guesses about exchange rates. In approach 3, it is necessary to make an assumption about the currency rate for each of the time periods in which the projects have NFVs. These additional assumptions make the appraisal more unsure given it is difficult to find out whether the size of the NPV is

---

[210] p. 133.

[211] If r varies over time, e.g., because it is estimated on the basis of the time structure of interest rates, then this can easily be incorporated into formula (9).

[212] See Chapter 4.1.

[213] Note: The initial calculation of NPV (foreign currency) should off course take the effects of economic and operating exposure into account.

caused by these additional assumptions about the interest rate or by the project itself. In approach 2, the project is appraised on its own terms, i.e., similar to approach 1, and only translated into the home currency afterwards. The translation of the NPV into the home currency can be supplemented by a sensitivity analysis with respect to the currency quotation to analyze the importance of variation in the currency to the investment.

3.2. Extending the Usability of the NPV Principle by the Means of Option Theory

As discussed in Chapter 4.1, the NPV principle is considered superior for evaluating and ranking investment proposals - at least within the area of finance. However, finance scholars also recognize that some aspects of an investment's economic value are not adequately captured by the NPV principle. In the NPV framework, an investment is viewed as fairly isolated,[214] and furthermore, an immediate acceptance/rejection is assumed. But not all investments share these features. Linked investments, those investments linked with future investment opportunities, are an example. And examples of linked investments are R&D-investments, market-entrance investments, and investments in cost and quality improvements. Similarly, some investment projects need not be accepted or rejected immediately since it may be possible to revise, e.g., to defer, expand or abandon, the investment project at a future time. These investments will henceforth be referred to as revisable investments. The opportunities (for future investments) and flexibility (to revise the investment) built into linked and revisable investments are not adequately captured by the NPV principle because they do not share its features. For example, the NPV framework uses fixed expected future values to calculate the NPV of an investment, but with respect to linked and revisable investments, their expected future values depends on the occurrence of a future event:

- if the future event is positive, then the next investment will be made or the investment will be expanded. In these incidences, the FV will be larger than the expected FV within the NPV framework due to the additional investment or the expansion of the investment.
- if the future event, on the other hand, is negative, then the next investment will not be made or the investment will be deferred/abandoned, and the negative FV, which otherwise would have occurred if the investment had been carried out as assumed in the NPVframework, will be avoided.

It is important to note the asymmetry in the FV's in each of the two states above; there is a positive value and a limited (if any) negative value. This asymmetry implies that the value of investment will not be affected as much by a high degree of uncertainty (i.e., risk), with respect to the occurrence of the future event, as would

---

[214] If a new investment affects the cash flow accruing from another investment (e.g., a machine which now produces another product and hereby generates cash flow) this should naturally be taken into account in the calculation of the NPV of the new investment.

be the case within the NPV framework, where risk normally is incorporated by raising the discount rate, which subsequently lowers the NPV of the investment.

With respect to the linked investment, the initial investment may have a negative NPV, but this is a precondition for carrying out the future investments, which may have a potential positive NPV. To make a correct evaluation of these investments, it is necessary not only to consider the NPV of the initial investment, as is done within the NPV framework, but also to consider the value of future investment opportunities. The value of opportunities arising from linked as well as revisable investments can be calculated using option theory. In the literature, opportunities arising from linked investment are normally referred to as »growth options« or »real options«, whereas opportunities arising from revisable investment are referred to as »operating flexibility«, even if these opportunities also are options.

From traditional option theory, it is known that an option is defined as the right, not the obligation, to buy or sell[215] a specific asset (the underlying »security«) at a specific price (the exercise price) at a specified date (the exercise date).[216] Within the framework of growth options/real options/operating flexibility,[217] the understanding of *the underlying »security«* as well as *the exercise price* varies from the ones known from traditional option theory. As expressed by Kester (1993):[218]

»The »security« underlying the discretionary investment opportunity...is actually the bundle of assets, tangible and/or intangible, that constitutes the opportunity in question. The growth option's »exercise price« is the cash outlay necessary to acquire the assets.«

When the NPV pattern (i.e., the PV at different points in time less the cash outlay necessary to acquire the asset) of the discretionary investment opportunity is estimated, then the growth option value can be calculated quite easily using a binomial model.[219] Recall the asymmetry in the growth option's value, as discussed

---

[215] A call option is the right to buy and a put option is the right to sell.

[216] An option with these characteristics is an European option. If it were possible to exercise the option at any time before a specific date, then the option would be an American option.

[217] Hereafter, the term »growth option« includes »growth options«,»real options« and »operating flexibility«.

[218] p. 189.

[219] The binomial model calculates the growth option value using only simple arithmetic. It is also possible to use the Black-Scholes option pricing formula. Because the Black-Scholes option pricing formula assumes continuous trading on the market, it is possible with this formula to price the option at any point in time up to the exercise date. With the binomial pricing model, it only possible to calculate the option price for each of the possible outcomes in each of the periods. However, as it is possible to make the periods extremely short, the Black-Scholes formula can be seen as a boundary case of the binomial model. Because of this and because the Black-Scholes formula is not as easy to understand intuitively as the binomial model is, it will not be presented here.

above; this asymmetry limits the lower bound to zero as opposed to the investment, the NPV pattern of which can be negative.[220] This asymmetry is utilized in the binomial model. The calculation of the growth option value starts in the last period, i.e., at the exercise date, at which time the value of the growth option is equal to the NPV of the investments, if this is greater than zero, otherwise the value of the growth option is equal to zero. By using the option values at the exercise date as input in a simple calculation, it is possible to calculate the value of the growth option in the previous period. The only data needed in addition to the data already presented for this calculation (i.e., the NPV pattern of the investment and the values of the growth options at the exercise date) is the risk-free rate of return.[221]

Figure 4.1 presents an example of how the value of a one-period growth option is calculated.[222]

[220] Another effect of this asymmetry is that the value of the growth option will always be larger than or equal to the value of the investment's NPV. The value of the growth option will be larger than the NPV of the investment at any time before the growth option is exercised, and the value of the growth option will be equal to the NPV of the investment when the growth option is exercised. For a graphical illustration of this, see Appendix B.

[221] As opposed to the NPV-principle - which includes the cost of risks in the rate of return - the rate used for calculating the value of options is the *risk-free* rate of return. Note that the factor by which the underlying asset rises/falls in the next period can be calculated from the NPV pattern. However, in Figure 4.1 the approach has been the opposite. The factor is just assumed to be 10% for both possible outcomes, and the NPV pattern in the second stage is calculated on this basis.

[222] The formula used to calculate the value of the growth option in stage 1 is presented in Appendix C.

Figure 4.1: Calculation of the value of a growth option using a simple binomial model

The NPV Pattern of the Investment (in mill.U.S.$)

The Growth Option Value of the Investment (in mill.U.S.$)

DATA & CALCULATIONS:

Stage 1:

PV of expected cash inflow:	99
Capital outlay:	100
NPV stage 1:	-1

Stage 2:
gain/loss in PV of expected cash inflow from prior success/failure: 10%

i.e., NPV (prior success): $99 \cdot (1+10\%) - 1 = +8.9$

NPV (prior failure): $99 \cdot (1-10\%) - 1 = -10.9$

Stage 2:
Value of growth option = max{NPV; 0}

Stage 1:
Value of growth option =

$$\frac{8.9 \cdot (1+0.05-0.9)+0 \times (1.1-1-0.05)}{(1+0.05) \cdot (1.1-0.9)}$$

$= 6.3571 \approx 6.4$

Note: risk free rate = 5%

An example of the value of a multiple period growth option is calculated and presented in Appendix C.

In the NPV framework, the investment presented in Figure 4.1 would not be accepted since the NPV is a negative U.S.$1,000,000. However, if the NPV framework is extended with option theory, then the result would be different. In this case, the value of the investment would be composed of two elements (see also Trigeorgis (1995)[223] and Kester (1993):[224]

1. the NPV of the investment's expected cash flow and
2. the value of the growth option(s).

[223] p. 2.

[224] p. 189.

In the extended NPV framework, the value of the investment presented in Figure 4.1 is a positive U.S.$5,400,000.[225] However, in the extended NPV framework, a positive value is not interpreted to mean immediate implementation of the investment is recommended as it would in the traditional NPV framework, because an implementation of the investment, in the first case, is the same as exercising the growth option and thus bringing its value to zero.[226] Under the assumption that more value is preferable to less value, this apparently implies that undertaking an investment (i.e., exercising the growth option) should be deferred as long as possible. For growth options, as opposed to traditional options, this implication is not always valid. The reasons why the exercise of a growth option should not necessarily be deferred as long as possible are to be found in two characteristics of growth options, which distinguish them from traditional options. As Kester (1993) says:[227]

1. »The holder of a call option on a security has the luxury of an exclusive right to the exercise of his or her particular option. The right cannot be abrogated legally by others. Competition for the investment opportunity held by the call option owner is nonexistent. In contrast, such a fully protected right to exercise a particular investment opportunity is not generally available to the holder of a growth option.«
2. »....growth options are not likely to be tradable at low cost in an efficient market.«

The first characteristic of the growth option, referred to in point 1 above, suggests that similar[228] or substitute growth option[229] may be available to other companies and therefore erode the value of the growth option. And since an efficient market does not likely exist, as implied by point 2 above, the erosion cannot be escaped by selling the option to others. Exercising a growth option early is a valid solution to

---

[225] The value of the investment is equal to:
U.S.$5,400,000 – U.S $ -1,000,000 + U.S.$6,400,000.

[226] If the value of the investment, i.e., the NPV value + the growth option value, had been negative, then the approach would have been the same as that using the traditional NPV framework, and the investment would have been abandoned.

[227] pp. 192-193.

[228] For example, opportunities to enter a new market, opportunities to expand (i.e., to build a new/larger factory and/or to hire more employees) and opportunities to switch output or input may be available to the whole industry, some of the competitors, or even some of the potential new entrants.

[229] Even if a company holds a legally-protected growth option, e.g., a patented product or production technology; it may be possible for a competitor to hold substituting growth options, i.e., a growth option that makes it possible to produce a substituting product or to make their production more efficient by alternative production technologies.

the anticipation of the erosion of the value of a growth option, according to Kester (1993) *if and only if:*[230]

»...the cost of killing the growth option is equal to or less the loss of the growth option value that would otherwise transpire.«[231]

In this respect, it should nevertheless be noted that, in the extended NPV framework, a positive extended NPV for an investment is still a prerequisite.

To summarize: An investment's extended NPV is equal to its NPV plus the value of its growth option(s).[232] The investment's NPV is calculated according to formula (9), and the investment's growth option value is calculated according to Appendix C. In the extended NPV framework, the investment decision rules can be formulated as follows:

1. if the extended NPV is negative, then the investment should be disregarded
2. if the extended NPV is positive, the investment should be deferred as long as possible *unless* the value of the growth option is anticipated to erode due to the action of competitors. *Then* the investment should be carried out immediately *if and only if* the cost of killing the growth option is equal to or less than the loss of the growth option value that would otherwise transpire.

4. Assessment of the NPV Research Programme

As a research programme, the NPV research programme differs from most other research programmes in that it consists almost solely of logical theories - at least the extent to which the NVP research programme is presented here. The hard core of the NPV research programme consists - as do many other research programmes - of a logical theory, in this incidence the NPV principle. What makes this research programme different from most other research programmes is the protective belt, since it does not contain any empirical theories, i.e., theories that make empirical postulates about actual relationships in the definite and directly observable reality. The protective belt of the NPV research programme gives directions on how to apply and extend the NPV principle, but it does not make any empirical postulates nor does it concern itself with the validity of the NPV principle, i.e., whether the investment decision turns out to be correct when the directions are followed. The lack of empirical postulates is quite interesting when considering that the sole purpose of applying the NPV principle to an investment is to predict the future, i.e., whether the investment will turn out to be profitable or not. If the estimation of

[230] p. 195.

[231] Note that an early killing, i.e., exercise of the growth option, may also have positive side effects, e.g., learning effects. These side effects should also be included in the calculations when deciding whether or not to exercise the growth option early.

[232] Note: several growth options may be connected to a specific investment.

future cash flows is not based on an empirical theory, the estimation will also be ad hoc. From a theoretical point of view, the use of ad hoc assumptions is rather unfortunate - a well-corroborated theory is preferred,[233] and this is yet another reason for developing empirical theories within the protective belt of the NPV research programme.

Among the criticism most commonly expressed by practitioners against the NPV principle is the difficulty of predicting an investment's cash flows far out in the future.[234] Some have tried to overcome this problem either by disregarding cash flows appearing after a certain period[235] or by assuming constant or increasing growth rates of the cash flow after a certain time horizon, e.g., five years. Others have tried to overcome this problem by supplementing the NPV principle with varying strategic analyses. It is my opinion, however, rather than supplementing the NPV principle with various, i.e., ad hoc, strategic analyses, it would be much more fruitful to reconcile the extended NPV principle with an empirical theory, e.g., a strategically-based theory that can postulate which investments to make under which circumstances. If such theory or theories are developed within the NPV research programme's protective belt, it is quite likely that the problems in applying the NPV principle[236] would be solved in given time, although it would be necessary to extend the current hard core with option theories[237] in order to capture the aspects of investments with which the NPV principle cannot adequately cope. If empirical theories are developed within the protective belt, then Lakatos predicts that a rivalry will occur among them and that the theories that are least corroborated will be eliminated, or falsified, leaving us with the best corroborated theories for guiding the investment appraisal process.

Within the framework of Lakatos' MSRP, it is not possible to assess the NPV research programme before such empirical theories are developed since the MSRP framework focuses solely on the development in empirical prediction of a research

---

[233] See Chapter 1.3.

[234] Note, it is widely - but wrongly - believed that precise estimates of investments' actual cash flows are needed in the NPV analysis, but in fact: »DCF calculations [i.e., the NPV principle; author's note] do not call for accurate forecasts, however, but for accurate assessment of the mean of possible outcomes.« Myers (1984), p. 133).

[235] If the scrap value of the investment is not incorporated into the NPV calculation, this would be the same as applying the DPB model, an approach not recommended by finance scholars due to the ad hoc nature of this model. See Chapter 4.1.

[236] According to Myers (1984), problems can arise when applying the NPV principle and estimating the cross-sectional links between projects and projects' impact on future investment possibilities is also areas.

[237] See Chapter 4.3.2.

programme when a research programme is assessed.[238] Thus, we can only conclude three things: that the NPV research programme is the dominant research programme within the area of finance; it is highly esteemed among finance scholars; and it is widely used by practitioners, although with some problems. In terms of Lakatos' MSRP, the NPV research programme may still be characterized as an emerging research programme despite its age. And even if it is not possible to appraise the NPV research programme due to its lack of empirical predictions, it certainly cannot be characterized as falsified, because the work on it still continues.

[238] See Lakatos' distinction between progressing, stagnation and degeneration problem shifts/research programmes in Chapter 1.3.2.

CHAPTER 5

Exploring Actual Acquisition Appraisal used by the Acquiring Companies

In Chapter 4, the conclusion was drawn that, although the NPV principle is highly recognized by finance scholars, the research programme still faces some problems. These problems include those of applying the NPV principle to some types of investments, the misapplication of the NPV principle, and the lack of empirical predictions in the NPV research programme. The problem of applying the NPV principle to some types of investments has been solved theoretically by extending the NPV principle with option theory. However, the two latter types, which are of a more empirical nature, still remain to be solved.

According to Popper's scheme of the scientific process,[239] the critical rationalist response to these empirical problems would be to propose one or several bold tentative theories. But Popper does not specify any method by which to generate such new theories. In fact, Popper does not care how new theories are obtained;[240] rather he believes that every discovery, i.e., tentative theory, contains an irrational element. So, the problem of »jumping« from the »problem« to the »tentative theory« still exists. However, Popper does stress that a good approach for a young scientist hoping to make discoveries is to study the problem situation of the day and to benefit from the knowledge already developed in that area.[241]

Up to this point in the book, the »problem« outlined above has only been examined from a theoretical point of view. But because the »problem« focuses on a number of empirical problems, it would be relevant also to explore and try to understand the problem from an empirical point of view, i.e., from the practitioners' point of view. Hopefully, such an empirical exploration could reveal some additional aspects, which a new tentative theory could include to its advantage. Furthermore, it would also be relevant to explore project interactions and growth options empirically to gain further understanding of when project interactions might destroy

---

239 See especially footnote 22, but also Chapter 1.3.1 in general.

240 What matters to Popper is that the generated theories are open to critical examination and refutation, i.e., that they are scientific in a Popperian sense.

241 See Chapter 1.3.1.

or create synergy effects, how growth options can be identified or created, and under which circumstances the value of growth options might be increased or decreased. Such knowledge may be useful in the creation of a tentative empirical theory, which could be helpful in the prediction of the cash flow needed as input in the extended NPV framework, i.e., in the application of the extended NVP principle.[242]

Thus, the purpose of this chapter is to explore the above-mentioned aspects of investment appraisal to gain further understanding of the problems involved when applying the NPV principle from an empirical point of view. Since the focus of this book is on Danish foreign acquisitions companies, this will be the type of investment examined in this chapter.

The first section of this chapter presents the specific research questions addressed in this chapter, along with the two applied methods - a multiple case study and a questionnaire. The research questions are, then, examined in the second section of this chapter where different aspects of the acquisition appraisal used by acquiring companies will be explored. This second section is divided into three subsections. Each one focuses on a part of the acquisition process. And each one deals with the aspects of that particular part of the process that is important to the appraisal of the investment, i.e., the acquisition. The findings and the understanding gained in this section will hopefully point towards those aspects a new tentative theory should include.

1. Presenting the Research Questions and the Applied Methods

This part of the book focuses on acquisition appraisal from the acquiring companies' perspective. So far, acquisition appraisal has been dealt with from a theoretical point of view and on a very general level, i.e., investment appraisal in general. Starting in this chapter, the focus will again be turned towards international acquisitions. In this section, the specific research questions addressed in this part will be presented, along with the two methods which have been applied for examining these research questions.

The predominant research question in this part of the book can be formulated as follows:

R.Q. 1: *How do acquiring companies appraise a potential target?*

This research question is put forward because empirical information is needed to gain further understanding of the empirical problems[243] facing the NPV research

[242] Recall from Chapter 4 that neither the NPV principle nor the scholars recommending how the NPV principle is to be applied give advice on the prediction of future cash flow. This has been left totally in the hands of those using the NPV principle.

[243] That is, the misapplication of the NPV principle, the lack of empirical predictions in the NPV research programme and how growth option investments actually are appraised empirically.

programme so that a new, tentative theory can be created to mitigate some of these empirical problems. The research question can be divided into a number of subquestions, each of which more specifically addresses one of the empirical problems needed to be explored:[244]

R.Q. 1.a: *Which methods are applied in the acquisition appraisal?*
R.Q. 1.b: *How are the methods applied?*
R.Q. 1.c: *Which aspects were considered to be important to the appraisal?*
R.Q. 1.d: *In what areas did the appraisal turn out to be wrong?*

In the empirical examination of these research questions, special emphasis will be placed on the »project interactions« and »growth options« of the investment to the extent these are present in the examined investment. Special emphasis has been placed on »project interactions« because much of the strategy literature on acquisitions motivates acquisition activity in some form of synergy effect, and if some form of synergy is expected in an acquisition, then the applied method should be able to incorporate this synergy, i.e., the project interaction, into the appraisal of the acquisition. Similarly, the reason for placing special emphasis on growth options is that the applied appraisal method should be able to handle growth options in the appraisal.

Two exploratory studies, a multiple case study[245] and a questionnaire, were conducted by the author to examine the research questions presented above.

The case study method was found to be an appropriate research strategy because the purpose of the research question was to explore the acquisition appraisal process within its real-life context. In the multiple case study the applied unit of analysis (or »case«) is the acquiring company's acquisition appraisal, i.e., its investment decision.

The initial research strategy was to use the same sample of acquisitions as was used in the event study.[246] Using this strategy , acquisitions with both positive and negative abnormal returns were selected for the case studies. In this way, the case studies would presumably consist of both successful and less successful acquisitions.[247]

---

[244] Note that the research questions, 1.a to 1.d, all address either the operationalization of the models or the validity of the models' statements, i.e., they are all examining whether the applied theories/methods/approaches are working in real life application. This is the only way to »test« logical theories empirically. See Chapter 13.1.

[245] »A case study is an empirical inquiry that • investigates a contemporary phenomenon within its real-life context, especially when • the boundaries between phenomenon and context are not clearly evident.« Yin (1994), p. 13.

[246] That is, the sample labelled »all acquirers« in Chapter 3.2.2. This sample consists of 42 acquisitions.

[247] The assumption is here that the stock market's reactions to acquisition announcements are unbiased. See Chapter 3.3. The original intention was to use the information collected in the case studies for the test of the unbiasedness hypothesis in Chapter 3.3.

Following this initial approach, contact[248] was made with the five companies in the subsample »major acquirers« and with the six companies in the subsample »other acquirers« having the three highest and lowest abnormal returns, respectively.[249] However, because the number of companies willing to participate was very limited, it was necessary to discard the initial research strategy. Subsequently, contact was made with all the companies in the sample »all acquirers«. In the end, using this approach, four companies agreed to participate in the case study.

The number of companies agreeing to participate in the case study was clearly less than initially anticipated. However, as the purpose of the case study is to gain further understanding of the empirical problems in the acquisition appraisal process and to create a tentative theory based - at least partly -on this insight, it is not necessarily the number of companies actually participating which is important. Rather, it is the honesty and boldness of the information passed on by the interviewed persons, in combination with the number of problems, success and failures he or she perceived or experienced in the acquisition appraisal process, that is important in this type of study. With respect to how to assess the honesty and boldness of the interviewed persons, the approach followed in the interview process rather ressembled the approach expressed by one of the interviewees, a manager with ISS International Service Systems A/S (ISS), in their acquisition appraisal process:[250]

»In the preliminary investigation, one has to believe the seller. In the course of the due diligence process, this belief should be verified.«

That is, one starts out with the belief the interviewed persons are telling the truth, and subsequently try to corroborate this belief throughout the interview process.[251] Information that is doubtful should be discarded. However, in the experience of this study, neither the lack of honesty nor boldness was a problem once the interviewed had accepted the interview. Thus, it was the number of problems, successes and failures perceived or experienced by the interviewed person in the acquisition appraisal process that became the critical issue in this study. Because these perceptions or experiences partly depended on the number of acquisitions in which the interviewed person had participated, it was decided that all foreign acquisitions in which the interviewed person had participated would be included rather than

---

248 A formal letter presenting the project and requesting an interview was sent to the person in the company believed responsible for the acquisition and/or the acquisition appraisal.

249 The sample »all acquirers« was divided into the two subsamples, »major acquirers« and »other acquirers«, in Chapter 3.2.2 . For further details about these samples, see Chapter 3.2.2.

250 This quotation, as well as all other quotations throughout Chapter 5, was translated by the author.

251 To the extent it is possible to use multiple sources of evidence this will of course increase the validity of the study.

limiting the interview to only those acquisitions included in the event study.[252] Quite fortunately, it turned out that two of the interviewed persons had participated in foreign acquisitions previously in their career in industries other than the one they were employed in at the time of the interview. Because they were willing to contribute their experiences from these acquisitions, it was decided that four companies were enough to build the mulitple case study on.

Among the four companies agreeing to participate, both subsamples, »major acquirers« and »other acquirers«, were represented.[253] Only one of the four companies, ISS,[254] appears by name in this book. An exception was made in Chapter 5.2.2, which deals with acquisition appraisal methods applied and for which full anonymity was preserved for discretionary reasons.

Interviews were made with six persons in the four companies, and to construct validity in the case studies, these persons have all either reviewed and approved a draft of the case study report or approved the relevant part of the case study used in Chapter 5.2.[255] All the persons interviewed belonged to the highest or second highest rank of management. However, for discretionary reasons and in agreement with the interviewed persons, all of the interviewed persons will be referred to as »manager«.

Because information was needed for the test of the unbiasedness hypothesis in Chapter 3.3 and because this information could not be obtained through the case studies, a questionnaire was constructed. It was sent out to the companies in the »all acquirers« sample, covering all 42 acquisitions. Due to the small number of participants in the case studies, a number of questions were included in this questionnaire to supplement - and perhaps extend - the information obtained in the case studies.

Information, in addition to that obtained in the case study, about methods used in acquisition appraisal, was especially warranted given the assumption that most acquirers use the same method for all their acquisitions. In this respect, it was of interest to find out if a number of different methods (financial, accounting as well as strategic) had been used to appraise the acquired company, and if so, how much

---

[252] Abandoning this limitation is not particularly important for the exploratory study in this chapter as the study's purpose is to gain insight for the creation of a tentative theory. It would, however, be important if the results should be used for testing the unbiasedness hypothesis. But this problem was solved in Chapter 3.3 by using another approach to obtain the necessary data. See Chapter 3.3.

[253] Note that the distinction between »major acquirers« and »other acquirers« was made on the basis of the number of acquisitions each of the acquirers conducted in the examined period. See Chapter 3.2.2. Thus, acquirers belonging to the sample »other acquirers« may have conducted several acquisitions over the years and they may also have had a more or less detailed strategy with respect to these acquisitions.

[254] ISS International Service Systems A/S (ISS) has a very open attitude towards researchers. As a result of this, ISS has been the topic of many case studies. See, e.g., Strandskov (1994) p. 423fn and Ackenhusen (1993).

[255] In the latter instance, the interview was recorded on a tape recorder.

importance had been assigned to the employed models. The timehorizon most commonly used was also examined.

As a supplement to the multiplecase study, the questionnaire also included a number of questions, about acquisition motive, acquirer's experience in making acquisitions and with the acquisition country, as well as a number of »statements« requiring comments (mostly about the integration phase and success of the acquisition). The questions addressing acquisition motive were constructed on the basis of the motives most commonly referred to in the literature[256] as well as on findings from the case study interviews. The »statements« in the questionnaire addressing the integration phase were constructed on the basis of the case studies, whereas the »statements« addressing the success of the acquisition were adapted from Hunt et al. (1987)[257].

Finally, a number of more factual questions about the target were included in the questionnaire because knowledge of the target companies was very limited due to the lack of public statistics in this area. These questions requested information about industrial sector, ownership structure, relative size to acquirer and motive for selling.[258]

2. Exploring Different Aspects of the Acquiring Companies' Acquisition Appraisal

In this section, results of the two investigations, i.e., the multiple case study and the questionnaire, exploring the acquiring companies' acquisition appraisal process, are presented.

The acquisition process can be viewed as consisting of three parts: the targeting and planning phase, the appraisal and negotiation phase, and the integration phase. All three phases contain elements important to acquisition appraisal.

In the targeting and planning phase, the target is identified. In this phase, the acquisiton motive is especially important to acquisition appraisal. For example, if the acquisition motive is an expectation of possible synergy effects, then a certain amount of attention should be placed on project interactions in the acquisition appraisal.

The appraisal and negotiation phase contains two steps. First, the consequences of the acquisition are appraised by the acquirer to find the maximum price, or a price range, to pay for the target. Second, the acquisition of the target is negotiated. In this phase, this investigation concentrates on those aspects expected to elucidate the research question proposed in Chapter 5.1. Negotiations are also of interest because

---

256 Trautwein (1990) and Weston et al. (1990), pp.425-426.

257 p .61.

258 The procedure for distributing the questionnaire was presented in Chapter 3.3.1.

an appraisal should include an assessment of how much the target company's owners expect to get paid for the target company. Thus, it is during the negotiation period that the acquirers discover whether the appraisal, with respect to the owners' demands, is realistic or not.

Finally, in the integration phase, intentions vis à vis the acquisition have to be carried into effect, and thus, this phase serves as a »test« of the validity of the appraisal.

The phases of acquisition mentioned above will be dealt with in turn in the following subsections. Here, the findings of the two empirical investigations will be presented. It has been chosen to present the findings of the two investigations simultaneously given the purpose of this chapter (i.e., to explore the different aspects affecting an acquisition appraisal process). Thus, the presentation of the empirical findings is structured accordingly, that is, focusing on the aspects following the phases of the acquisition process as outlined above.

2.1. The Targeting Phase : Strategies, Motives and Coincidences

The multiple case study showed that many paths lead to an acquisition. Quite a number of acquisitions resulted from an active acquisition strategy, other acquisitions resulted from a more defensive nature, and finally some acquisitions resulted from mere coincidence or unsolicited applications.

Although all the companies participating in the studies had a more or less comprehensive acquisition strategy, the strategy was far from always followed. However, one company, namely ISS, differed from the other acquirers: it used a very detailed acquisition strategy and adhered to it. The local management of ISS' subsidiaries constantly screens their market for potential targets.[259] This screening is considered a part of the local managers' job of keeping up-to-date with the competitors and their market positions.

Generally, ISS seeks three types of acquisitions: *market entry acquisitions*, for obtaining a base in a new market; *filler acquisitions*, for expanding and consolidating the market; and *mid-size acquisitions*, for expanding and consolidating the market through larger companies than those acquired in filler acquisitions. Market entry acquisitions are relatively large in size due to their purpose and are often among the 3-5 largest companies in that particular market. Filler acquisitions are small acquisitions in which ISS mainly focuses on cleaning contracts and on cleaning personnel. As the name indicates, mid-size acquisitions are companies, whose size is between that found in market entry acquisitions and filler acquisitions.

The focus on cleaning contracts and on cleaning personnel already in the targeting phase is quite evident since these two elements are preconditions for the value creation in acquisitions in this line of business. A solid contract and customer base in the target company warrants an earning potential for ISS to build on. Similarly,

---

[259] The coming new president of ISS, Mr. Waldemar Schmidt, recently announced in the Danish media that, in the future, ISS will concentrate on organic growth rather than growth by acquisitions as it has done so far.

a low turnover in personnel is desirable, not only in the acquisition situation, but also once the acquisition has been fully carried out, since a high turnover leads to high costs and instability in the cleaning teams.

The local ISS subsidiary is responsible for making filler acquisitions in its market. However, when an ISS subsidiary wants to make an acquisition, ISS headquarters requires the subsidiary to prepare a clear acquisition strategy plan before permission will be given to go ahead with the acquisition. Included in such an acquisition strategy plan should be answers to the following questions:

* what is the purpose of this particular acquisition?
* which expectations need to be fulfilled?
* how is the target to be adapted to/integrated in the ISS subsidiary?

Thus, ISS requires that thorough consideration be made about the integration of the potential target already in the targeting phase since, in ISS' experience, the integration phase is one of the most critical steps in the acquisition process. As manager of ISS expressed it:

»How is a local manager supposed to know what to do with an acquired company *after* the acquisition if he doesn't know it before the acquisition?«

Another case company maintained a very active acquisition strategy that was carried out with all acquisitions made by this company. This company's overall corporate strategy was identical with its corporate strategy, namely to expand within one of its already well-established business areas as a means of supplementing or filling a hole in product assortment and of earning as much money as quickly as possible. The motive for this strategy was based on the idea that the company could better conduct investments within its own line of business than its stockholders could, given its knowledge of the business.

This company also actively sought potential acquisition targets on a continuous basis. In the screening process, all potential targets located in Europe were of interest, in principle, excepting targets located in Italy and to a certain extend also of eastern Europe. Potential targets in Italy was not considered due to this country's extend of black economy. Because the Italian culture in this respect is so different from the Danish, the company felt that it would not be able to control an Italian subsidiary sufficiently. Subsequently, the case company was not interested in making acquisitions in Italy. Eastern Europe was of lesser interest in the screening mainly because the number of relevant targets were very limited, but also because the acquirer felt that Treuhand's[260] demands for keeping the workforce intact for a certain period after an acquisition would cause too much delay in turning the target into an efficient and profitable company.

---

[260] Treuhand is the organization responsible for selling the previously state-owned companies in the former East Germany.

Contacts with potential targets were obtained through the case company's own knowledge of these, by other people in the industry, and by the use of investment bankers.

To fulfil its strategy of acquiring European companies within its core business and to earn as much money as quickly as possible, the case company established a target profile, which it used both in the screening process and in the evaluation of a target's potential. The target profile was based partly on experience from previous acquisitions made by this case company and partly on the manager's extensive acquisition experience from another line of industry. In addition to some very specific demands for a product and customer base, derived from the strategy of filling or supplementing the core business, the target profile consisted of the following:

1. The case company is only interested in buying profitable targets. This will limit potential targets to the more expensive ones, but as the manager stated:

»In our opinion, it is expensive to buy cheap.«

2. The target has to be well-managed since the case company's intention is to keep existing management. To the case company, several elements characterize a good target management: it has to be stable, it has to have excess management capacity, it has to be fluent in English, and it has to show an ability to generate profit. The second element is vital. It is the case company's experience that acquisitions not only call for extra resources, but also for extra management attention even if the case company only requires a few changes - mainly in the management control system - after the acquisition. Only few changes are usually required because the case company has a very decentralized structure. The motives for these demands are expressed by the manager of the case company in the following:

»We don't think we are super-managers who just can add a little »good management« to badly-managed companies. Acquisitions take time and excess management energy - even when well-managed companies are acquired.«

3. Only friendly acquisitions are made. This is a consequence of the wish to keep the current management of the target.[261]

The purpose of the target profile is to reduce the risk of making an unsuccessful acquisition. In this respect, acquisition experience is very valuable. But as the manager of the case company stated:

»Previous experience with acquisitions from other industries reduces the acquisition risk, however, it still takes two or three years before you know the industry specific acquisition risks.«

[261] Interestingly, this view was supported in a comment by a manager of one of the other companies participating the case study: »The Danish mentality is simply not towards hostile acquisitions.«

The preference for well-managed and profitable targets was also prevalent in the third company participating in the case study. As expressed by the manager interviewed:

»We would like to buy companies with a strong market position. They have to be well-managed and earn money. We don't want to buy companies with problems because we cannot run the company from Denmark. And if you have to change a whole layer of managers...well, it is a very slow process.«

Also this acquirer's overall strategy was very linked to its acquisition strategy, given that its purpose was to internationalize its core business through acquisitions over the next five to ten years in order to rank among the market leaders in Europe.[262] Once again, the focus of the active acquisition strategy was on core business and on well-managed, European targets.

Another of the case companies included in the case study had a more defensive acquisition strategy. This case company only acquired when it felt it necessary to preserve its market position in a specific market. As expressed by the interviewed manager:

»Typically, we have acquired one of our distributors for one of two reasons: either we did not feel that the specific market was serviced the way we wanted it - they simply *had* to be able to sell more - or the distributor's owners simply wanted to quit and you start thinking: what if a new owner is not able to run it properly? So our acquisitions have been directed by necessity and coincidence.«

But even for the acquirers who followed an active and well-defined acquisition strategy, there still occured a number of acquisitions through more coincidental circumstances. One of the interviewed managers related the following incidence that later led to an acquisition:

»It[263] occurred by mere coincidence. A letter was wrongly dispatched. It should have been sent to another company and . . . Well, it was a rather small company and not located in one of our high priority countries. But we had sold a bit in that country. So we responded to the letter. At that time, it was actually regarding a product joint venture.«

In addition to their stated acquisition strategies, some of the managers had guidelines they followed in the targeting phase. These quidelines were often based on their experience. These are reported by one of the interviewed managers in the following:

---

[262] For this reason, the screening was obviously limited to European targets.

[263] That is, the target company.

»There is this golden rule that you cannot buy a target that is larger than your own. Well, if your board lets you and you have the money for it, then of course you could. But in reality, you would not be able to control it adequately, and it is difficult for a small company to tell a larger company how to run their business. Therefore, there is a certain rhythm you have to follow. So if we could buy a company with a turnover of, say, two-thirds of our own, then that would be a big mouthful for us. Once you have acquired such a large target, then you have to spend a couple of years before you can move on to the next one.«

Interestingly, the importance of spending time integrating an acquisition before moving on to the next , as expressed in the above comment, was supported by one of the respondents to the questionnaire, who made the following comment in the questionnaire:

»The acquisition did not lead to the expected strengthening of the marketing side mainly because our focus shortly thereafter shifted to another, much larger acquisition in the same country.«

Another of the interviewed managers found that the amount of attention an acquirer is able to give to a target after an acquisition also needs to be considered in the targeting phase in order to select an appropriate target. As he stated:

»Focusing on core business just isn't enough; you also have to focus on the business system to see if the target will fit into your company. For example, take our former subsidiary, X. They were a good company with a rather large potential, but were rather small, and they did not fit into our business system. They felt that they had too little contact with our managers, that they got too little help and had to spend too much time making detailed budgets, strategy plans and so on. They simply did not fit into our business system - we were not the right parent company for them.«

As previously mentioned, the questionnaire also investigated the motives behind the acquisitions made by the companies in the sample »all acquirers«. The result of this investigation is shown in Table 5.1.

Table 5.1: Importance of acquisition motives, frequency table

Question 2.3: Please state the importance of the conditions below to your company at the time of the acquisition	Index: 1: of little importance; 5: of much importance					Average
	1	2	3	4	5	
	------number of responses------					
a. Access to an otherwise hard-to-access market	3	4	4	3	7	3.3333
b. Target's market knowledge	2	4	3	8	4	3.3810
c. Possibility of faster growth	0	1	2	8	10	4.2857
d. Possibility of synergies of scale or scope in production or marketing	0	3	2	12	4	3.8095
e. Expectations of increased stability in supply/ lower cost (raw materials, labor etc.)	4	4	9	2	2	2.7143
f. Access to technical knowledge, patents, technology etc.	6	5	5	3	2	2.5238
g. Possibility to buy a competitor	6	2	8	2	3	2.7143
h. Possibility to obtain a more stable sale	2	3	6	8	2	3.2381
i. Expectation of increased sale	0	0	3	10	8	4.2381
j. Expectation of increased productivity	3	1	7	8	2	3.2381
k. Access to good, foreign managers	6	6	5	3	1	2.3810
l. Wish to diversify (other business and products)	10	3	2	5	1	2.2381
m.Possibility of tax advantage	17	2	1	1	0	1.3333
n. Overcoming trade barriers	15	3	2	1	0	1.4762

Note: 42 questionnaires were sent out. 21 were returned and usable, leading to a 50% response rate.

As is evident from point (c) and (i) in Table 5.1, growth motives were among the predominant acquisitions strategies in this sample. The questionnaire also indicated, in points (d) and (l), a focus towards acquisitions in a core business rather than in one representing diversification. Finally, the questionnaire clearly showed that neither the possibility of tax advantage nor the possibility of overcoming trade barriers were of much importance in these foreign acquisitions.[264]

Having a clear acquisition strategy is one aspect to consider. Another aspect, however, concerns which target companies wind up on the market. In the questionnaire, one of the questions addressed the target companies' main motives for *selling* the target company. The answers to that question are shown in Table 5.2.

[264] See Table 5.1, points (m) and (n).

Table 5.2: Main motives of target company owners for selling their company

Question 1.5: Please state the main reason for why the target company is for sale	Number of responses	% of total
Generational change	6	28.57
Profitability or cash flow problems	5	23.81
The supply of new resources /Needed competencies for securing continued development and expansion of the target	5	23.81
Other reasons	5	23.81
Total*	21	100

* a total of 21 answers, equivalent to a 50% response rate.
Note: in the questionnaire it was possible to specify more than one motive for selling the target company. However none of the respondents used this possibility.

As is evident from Table 5.2, the three specified responses in Question 1.5 account for slightly more than three quarters of the motives for selling. The distribution of these responses, including »other reason«, is almost even, although there was a greater preference for the motive »generational change«. Interestingly, almost a quarter of the acquired targets indicated economic problems. This tendency conflicts with the acquisition strategies stated in the case studies: Companies participating in the case studies generally did not want to acquire companies with economic or managerial problems. It is not possible to identify whether this difference is the result of a willingness to part from a stated strategy once a good offer comes along or of a mismatch in representativity between the companies included in the case studies and the respondents of the questionnaire.

The questionnaire also examined a number of characteristics of the target companies. These are shown in Table 5.3.

Table 5.3: Characteristics of the target companies

Question 1.1: Please indicate if the target company was a:	Number of responses:	
Service company	1	
Trading company	7	
Manufacturing company	12	
Other	1	
Total*	21	
Question 1.2: Was the target company listed on the stock exchange?	Yes:	No:
	0	21
Question 1.3: Please indicate the ownership structure[265] of the target company:	Number of responses:	
Family ownership	13	
Diversified ownership (several owners, no individual holds the voting majority)	0	
Owned by another company (subsidiary or division)	5	
Other	3	
Total*	21	
Question 1.4: Please state size of target relative to that of your own company	No. of responses measured by:	
	a. turnover:	b number of employees
0 -5%	10	10
5 - 10%	5	3
10 - 25%	3	3
25 - 50%	2	2
> 50%	1	1
. (missing values)	0	2
Total*	21	21

* a total of 21 responses, equivalent to a 50% response rate.

[265] For definitions, see Chapter 3.2.2.

From Table 5.3, it is evident that the majority responding to the questionnaire had acquired manufacturing companies. A majority of the targets had family ownership, and none of the targets were listed on the stock exchange.[266] The size of the target acquired relative to the size of the acquirer was relatively small: in almost half of the acquisitions, the relative size was 5% or less, measured both in turnover and number of employees. Only one of the acquisitions was more than 50% larger than the acquirer, measured both in turnover and number of employees. This tendency seems to support the comment, made above by one of the interviewed managers in the case studies, about »the golden rule«: not to acquire a target larger than the acquiring company.

Previous acquisition experience is another aspect indicated by the case study as important to the acquisition process, especially in the targeting phase, because the experienced acquirer is then better able to sort potential targets. Table 5.4 shows the results of the questions examining acquirers' experience with foreign acquisition and with the acquisition country, respectively.

---

[266] In Chapter 3.2.1, testing of the predictions of Jensen's »free cash flow hypothesis« and Roll's »hubris hypothesis«, with respect to change in shareholder wealth of the target company, was discarded due to a lack of access to foreign stock market data. However Question 1.2. in Table 5.3 indicates that such tests hardly would have been possible anyway since the majority of target companies presumably would not have been listed.

Table 5.4: Acquirer's experience with acquisition country and activity prior to the acquisition

Question 2.1: Please specify how many acquisitions your company had conducted abroad in the five-year period prior to this acquisition:	Number of responses:	% of total:
None	5	23.81
1 - 2	6	28.57
3 - 5	3	14.29
> 5	7	33.33
Total	21	100
Question 2.2: Please specify the types of activity your company had in the country of the acquisition *prior* to the acquisition:	**Number of responses:**	**% of respondents conducting the specified activity prior to the acquisition**
No previous activity	3	14.29
Direct sale	7	33.33
Export through distributor	2	9.52
Export through own sales company	3	14.29
Own production	5	23.81
Something else e.g. licensing	3	14.29
Total*	23	

*Because a company may have several activities in the acquisition country, the total exceeds the number of respondents.

As is evident from Table 5.4, in more than half of the acquisitions, the acquirer had limited or no prior acquisition experience, i.e. they had made two or less foreign acquisitions prior to the acquisition in question. However, a third of the acquisitions were conducted by what may be characterized as experienced acquirers, i.e., they had previously made more than five foreign acquisitions. The predominant proportion of the acquirers (85.71%) had had some form of activity in the acquisition country prior to the acquisition in question. This prior experience with the acquisition country had presumably helped to reduce the cultural differences experienced during the acquisition process.[267]

But the acquirer's experience, both with making acquisitions and with the acquisition country, is not only important for the screening of relevant targets, but

[267] This observation harmonizes with the conclusions drawn in a seminal study by Johanson & Vahlne (1977): »We believe that lack of knowledge due to differences between countries with regard to, for example, language and culture, is an important obstacle to decision making connected with the development of international operations.« p. 26.

also for the appraisal of the target. The next subsection will explore this and the importance of other aspects in the appraisal and negotiation phase.

2.2. The Appraisal and Negotiation Phase: Calculating and Closing the Deal

Once a potential target has been identified, then the next phase of the acquisition process - the appraisal and negotiation phase - begins. This phase may be quite hectic in the »real« world because much may be happening at the same time. However, here we have the fortune of only being able to present one thing at a time and thus, for the purpose of clarity we will deal with the aspects and issues of importance to this phase in turn. This will be done under the following headings: *applied methods of appraisal, aspects important to the appraisal,* and *the negotiations and their influence on price.*

2.2.1. Applied methods of appraisal

In the questionnaire, there were two questions addressing both the methods or approaches used for appraising the target and the time horizon used for the appraisal, respectively. The answers to these questions are shown in Tables 5.5 and 5.6, respectively. Table 5.5 shows that cash flow models, accounting analysis including intrinsic value, and strategic analysis were the approaches most commonly used in the appraisal of the target company. Table 5.6 shows that the most commonly used time horizon was 6 years or less.

Table 5.5: Approaches used for the appraisal of the target company

Question 2.4: Please specify the approaches your company used for the appraisal of the target company and their importance:	Index. 1. of little importance; 5: of much importance					Number of respondents using the approach*	Weighted average
	1	2	3	4	5		
	number responding						
Cash flow models, net present value	-	-	1	11	2	14	4.07
Capitalized earnings/dividend	-	1	2	1	1	5	3.40
Price-earning ratio	-	-	-	5	-	5	4.00
Market value, stock price	-	-	-	-	-	0	-
Pay-back time	-	-	2	3	-	5	3.60
Intrinsic value	-	4	6	4	1	15	3.13
Substance value, liquidation value	-	1	1	1	-	3	3.00
Accounting analysis	-	-	-	4	7	11	4.64
Strategic analysis	3	-	2	4	6	15	3.67

* There were 19 respondents answering this question.

Table 5.6: Time horizon used for the appraisal

Question 2.5: Please state the time horizon most often used for the appraisal of the acquired company:	< 1 year	1-2 years	3-4 years	5-6 years	7-8 years	9-10 years	>10 years
	----------number responding----------						
	0	0	9	4	0	3	0

Note: the total number of respondents that answered this question was 16.

As is evident from Table 5.5, although indirectly, most companies use more than one approach in the appraisal of an acquisition target. On the basis of their answers to Questions 2.4 and 2.5, it was possible to classify the predominant proportion of the respondents into one of three groups, according to their applied methods of appraisal, its rank[268] and the time horizon used. The largest group of respondents (8) used three types of appraisal methods, namely, models belonging to the NPV research programme,[269] accounting-based models and strategic models. This group of respondents all used a 3-4 year time horizon. The second largest group of respondents (4) only used models belonging to the NPV research programme and accounting-based models. Three of the respondents in this group used a time horizon of 9-10 years and one used a time horizon of 3-4 years. The final group of respondents (3) only used strategic models, and none in this group specified their time horizon. The remaining 4 respondents fell outside these three groups, mainly due to their ranking of the applied methods of appraisal.

The grouping of respondents according to type of appraisal methods used, as evident in the questionnaire, was also partly evident in the case studies. Three of the companies in the case studies generally used models based on the NPV research programme, accounting-based models and strategic models in their appraisal. The ranking of these models, as well as the time horizon used, however, varied from company to company and with the type of acquisition.

One of the case study companies put most emphasis on its cash flow model. The expected cash flow for a target over a 10-year time horizon or less was estimated on a pre-tax basis.[270] The net present value of the cash flow was calculated using a 20% discount rate, approximately, and several sensitivity analyses were conducted with respect to consequences of changes in the assumptions as well as the probability of these changes. Quite interestingly, all possible synergy effects between the target and the acquirer were omitted from the calculations. This company was of the firm

[268] Note that the ranks are omitted in the following presentation, for clarity reasons.

[269] See Chapter 4 for further details about the NPV research programme.

[270] Due to some company-specific aspects, the company participating in the case study did not pay tax.

opinion that all synergies, at least with respect to production synergies, are much overrated, or as the manager stated:

»Synergies always come in smaller size and later than expected.«

This opinion was shared by another of the interviewed managers who in hindsight commented:

»In the real world, all things take a much longer time, don't get the volume as fast as expected, and perhaps costs incurred are higher than expected. So you have to be *very* - wouldn't an economist always say that - *very* cautious in incorporating synergy effects in your NPV - at least in the first couple of years after the acquisition. On the other hand, the decision is often motivated by strategy. That is, if you want a platform, this is what it costs. If you can justify the acquisition by the target's profit, that is fine. But this is not always possible, and then you have to believe that you are able to improve the profit over time. You should be able to do just that - otherwise, you should not have made the acquisition.«

The consistent disregard of synergies in the calculation of NPV was not followed by the other case study companies in this group,[271] as is evident from the following quotation of one of the interviewed managers:

»Their earnings looked really good, and we estimated what our products would be able to contribute to these earnings over a five-year period, and it looked unbelievably good. But then you also have to consider what it takes to have earnings like they[272] have now, and the question becomes, for how long can they keep the earnings this high? This is the difficult part, to estimate »how long those products will last,« and especially »how long they will last if they are not supplemented with new products«. We had to estimate what our product would do to the life of their product, to their assortment and to their turnover.«

Another of the case companies appraised the target company both on an integrated basis as well as on a stand alone basis, using a discounted cash flow analysis. The cash flow analysis was supplemented with a financial review of the target company, conducted mainly by local accountants and lawyers. Local accountants and lawyers were used for most of the acquisitions that were discussed by the interviewed persons in the multiple case study. These analyses were supplemented with, what the specific case company referred to as, »operational reviews«, i.e. analyses of target company characteristics that, in the case company's experience, would be important to the success of the acquisition and thus also important to the price.

One of the case companies did not use NPV based models, and subsequently this company did not fall into the same group as the three other companies mentioned above. As the interviewed manager noted:

---

[271] That is, those case study companies using three categories of appraisal models.

[272] That is, the target company.

»I think it is fine, if you have a number of controllers with nothing else to do, to let them make as many cash flow analyses as they like. But that does not take away the responsibility of the manager and the board of directors to do *their* job, that is - with their pencil - to calculate, in their own manner and in the way *they* think, whether this is a good acquisition or not.«

Thus, instead of spending time doing cash flow analyses, this case company concentrated both on analyses of a more strategic nature and on accounting analysis. The analysis of the target company's accounts was generally based on a five-year time horizon. When acquiring its distributors, this case company also disregarded synergy effects, i.e., goodwill, in its calculation of how much it should pay for the target company. As stated by the interviewed manager:

»The value of the target company is totally dependent on the target company being a distributor of our products. So in our opinion, the goodwill accumulated in the target company belongs to us. We don't want to pay for the specific goodwill in the agency that we have created for the distributor.«

In its acquisition of manufacturing companies, this case company did, however, expect to pay some goodwill in addition to the target's intrinsic value. In these acquisitions, the analysis of the accounts were supplemented with sales forecasts and analysis of the earnings. But the case company still did not use cash flow based models for these analyses.

The estimation of goodwill is often very difficult, and the final result can appear to be random, at least for business school scholars and as is suggested by the following quotation from one of interviewed managers at another of the case study companies:

»We started out by looking at the expected turnover and profit of the combined business, using our company's profit ratio. As a potential, that gave us an increase of approximately X millions in our turnover and Y millions in our profit over the next four years. Then we estimated that perhaps half of the additional turnover and profit was realistic.«

The strategic analyses conducted in the appraisal phase involves a check to see that the criteria by which the target should be selected in the screening phase[273] are actually present in the target company to the degree desired. However, a number of aspects, contained in many of the strategic analyses[274] conducted in the appraisal phase, are not included in the targeting phase. The most general of these will be presented in the following discussion.

---

[273] See also the acquisition strategies and screening criteria of the case study companies, presented in Chapter 5.2.1.

[274] That is, analysis of a more »strategic« nature.

2.2.2. *Aspects important to the appraisal*

Among the aspects important to the acquisition appraisal, several aspects were common for the case study companies. They included the target's commitments, the customer base and the target's operations. However, analyses involving these aspects were usually conducted *after* a letter-of-intent[275] had been signed because much of the information used in these analyses, first collected during the process of due diligence,[276] was very sensitive and valuable to competitors, a category which often includes the acquirer prior to the acquistion. In the letter-of-intent, the price or price level for the target company is often specified, although it is often negotiable to a certain extent after the due diligence process, depending on what the acquirer »finds« in his analysis of the target company. Furthermore, a number of so-called »walk away« clauses also appear often in the letter-of-intent. »Walk aways« are specified circumstances under which the acquirer can cancel the intent to acquire.

All of the case study companies put great emphasis on examination of the target's commitments. These commitments varied, of course, from target company to target company, but most often, they included contracts with employees, the pay and holiday pay of different employee groups, notice of termination and related compensation for different employee groups, and insurance policies. It is not surprising that these aspects were examined in all acquisitions included in the multiple case study, considering that all of the companies used external (local) accountants and/or lawyers.[277] The following quotation, made by one of the interviewed managers, bears witness to the idea that these aspects really are greatly important to acquisition appraisal:

»We find the use of a local lawyer very important in the assessment of contracts that the target company has already entered into, *especially* with respect to employment contracts. In many countries, it is very difficult to dismiss employees and to avoid unpleasant surprises. So we have made it a habit *always* to examine this aspect.«

The content of employee contracts used by foreign targets may perhaps be especially surprising to a Danish acquirer. As expressed by one of the interviewed managers:

»In Denmark, it is quite easy to dismiss employees. In other countries - and especially in Southern Europe - the employees are very protected by the national laws in this regard.«

An assessment of the target company's customer base and its growth potential was also included in most of the acquisition appraisals made by the case study companies. This aspect is especially important to service companies, like ISS, where

---

[275] Letter-of-intent is a contract specifying that the acquirer intends to buy the target company.

[276] The process of »due diligence« covers the examinations that the acquirer finds necessary to conduct in connection with an acquisition.

[277] These aspects are natural areas of interest for accountants and lawyers in a due diligence process.

the dependence between product and customer is strong.[278] An assessment of the customer base and its growth potential is also contained in ISS' analysis of contracts. However, because ISS' considerations in this respect were dealt with in Chapter 5.2.1, their appraisal will not be addressed in this respect any further here.

For some manufacturing companies also, it is necessary to assess the target company's customer base. As expressed by one of the interviewed managers:

»Our industry is a derived industry. So in order to increase sales, either new customers, an increase in customers' sales or new fields of application are needed. Thus, it is important to find trend-setting customer groups that have potential to expand. And in an acquisition situation, it is therefore relevant to assess the customer base and its growth potential.«

In instances where case study companies acquired a manufacturing company, an on-site examination of the production plants was also generally included in the appraisal. However, these on-site examinations often took place after the letter-of-intent had been signed. One of the case companies had their technicians visit the target company. The technicians assessed the technology of the production plants, the maintenance of these plants, and so on. They also made notes on hygiene and whether the workers were idle at their machines. This information could, later on, be used for rationalizing the acquisition, as the manager noted:

»Are, for example, 10 workers idle by the machines, then it will most likely be possible to reduce the work force after the company has been acquired. The saved wages mean that the investment in the acquisition will have a faster pay-back.«

Because environmental issues are becoming an increasingly important issue both with respect to customers and to public legislation, this aspect will also sometimes be necessary to include in the acquisition appraisal. The environmental issues were included in one case company's appraisal of an acquisition, where in fact a thorough environmental due diligence was conducted.

There have been cases where the appraisal is not limited to what the acquirer seeks to acquire. In one instance, a case study company wanted to acquire only that part of a target company that fit into its own core business. However, this was not possible, and it was necessary to both appraise and consider what to do with the other parts of the target company the acquirer did not really want. As the interviewed manager for that company said:

278 Services often have the characteristic of being produced and consumed at the same time.

»Actually, we were only interested in buying the Z business area; we were not at all interested in buying the other parts. But they[279] did not dare to sell this half of their company and risk getting stuck with the rest. So we had to buy it all. It was our strategy from the beginning that, once we had acquired it, we should resell the unwanted part. We did not even bother analyzing further to see if it was something we wanted to keep. It simply did not fit into our business. We had some concern as to whether we would be able to sell that part, but we were able to identify some potential buyers. But how we appraised it...Well, as I recall, we asked the potential buyers how much they would pay.«

Furthermore, one of the interviewed managers pointed out that appraisal of a target company often had to be conducted within a fairly short time horizon because a potential acquisition is often a very emotional situation for the target company's employees at all levels and also sometimes for the owners.

Various aspects, including those mentioned above and others of a similar kind, can be used by an acquiring company in its appraisal of a potential target company. The assessment of these aspects, whether financial or stategic, may or may not be incorporated in a formal model used to find the appropriate price to pay for a target company. However, when it comes to the actual price paid, it is not necessarily appraisal models that are most important. As expressed by one of the interviewed managers:

»These models[280] are very fine, but the real world is one big horse trade!«

Quite interestingly, this manager was not the only manager interviewed who referred to negotiations as a horse trade! And this leads to the next and final issue in the appraisal and negotiation phase: the negotiations and their influence on the price.

2.2.3. Negotiations and their influence on the price

As previously mentioned,[281] the case companies made only friendly acquisitions. In the negotiations concerning a friendly acquisition, the establishment of a mutual trust between negotiators representing the target company and the acquirer is very important, as reflected in the following comments made by several of the interviewed managers:

»The personal relationships, if you are able to establish them, and to obtain respect for each others competencies and for what you want to do with the target company. Those were the crucial elements in this situation.«[282]

---

[279] That is, the owners.

[280] Referring to the models used in the appraisal.

[281] See Chapter 5.2.1.

[282] That is, the negotiation of a specific acquisition deal.

»In some countries we have lost the acquisition to others...because the first step[283] is the most difficult one.«

». . .because you must get those people[284] to establish a *tremendous* confidence in you when they are close to retirement and would be very well off economically no matter whom they sold to. But they sold their company to us - and for a cheaper price than that offered by others - because they believed that we were decent people, that we only wanted the best for the company, and that we were able to do it and were not just making empty promises.«

The establishment of mutual trust and understanding in the negotiations, and the differences in cultural background between the negotiating teams of the target and potential acquirers, can be very important for whom the target decides to sell to.[285] One of the case study companies acquired a target that previously had been negotiating with a - also foreign - company they had been cooperating with at that time. However, this other acquirer was just a bit too eager, so they ended up losing the deal. As expressed by one of the interviewed managers:

». . .it was simply too much for them.[286] X[287] was too pushy, so they decided not to sell to X.«

Another of the managers interviewed put great emphasis on having a certain amount of cultural familiarity with the target's negotiators :

»The further you are away from your cultural background, the less you can trust your intuition. If you are speaking with someone from a distant country, it is much more difficult to judge if he is telling the truth or not and whether he has understood what you are trying to communicate.«

Intuition is also used in the negotiations to »feel« what is and is not important to the target company's owners in order to close the deal in one's own favor. In some acquisitions, the continuance of the target and/or its name can be a crucial point in the negotiations, presumably most often when the target company's owners are emotionally connected to their company.[288] In one of the acquisitions covered in the case study, this particular aspect turned out to be decisive for closing the deal in their favor. The acquirer agreed in the letter-of-intent to continue the target company under its current name and stated intentions to strengthen the target company in order to secure its turnover and profit. These guarantees were so important to the

---

283 That is, the establishment of contact, confidentiality and trust.

284 That is, the managers and owners of a specific target company.

285 Note that the focus is still on friendly acquisitions.

286 That is, the target's owners.

287 That is, the other acquirers.

288 For example, because the target company is family-owned and has been so for decades or even centuries, or because the owner and manager has established the company himself.

target company's owners that the deal was closed at a considerably lower price than what other acquirers had offered. The other acquirers bidding on this specific target company were close competitors to the target in the acquisition country, and they had no intention of making the kind of promises made by the Danish acquirer.

Tax issues can many times also be important for the target company's owners because specific constructions of the deal can sometimes ease the taxation of the target's owners. One of the interviewed managers felt that often an exorbitant amount of time was spent in the negotiations on tax issues.

A general tactic in the negotiations seemed to be for the acquirers to hold as much information back for as long as possible. Nevertheless, one of the case study companies used an alternative and very open strategy, with respect to presenting both the price and the foundation on which the price was obtained to the target's owners. In the words of the interviewed manager:

»We present the price to the target's owners as fast as possible and tell them that the appraisal is based on the target's expected cash flow and a yield on the invested capital of X%. We inform them this early about the price because we don't want to waste time and energy on negotiations and analysis if the price difference between buyer and seller is too big to make a deal. The target company's owners often focus on equity when they want to sell their company, and this is yet another reason for informing them about our appraisal. Furthermore, it is our experience that the owners are not always familiar with their company's strong and weak sides, so we often contribute a new view on these.«

In the negotiations, both parties try to win as many of their own demands and still reach a final agreement. Sometimes, however, there will be a gap between the two parties desiderata. In this situation, one of the interviewed managers gave the following advice:

»When negotiations break down due to a relatively small price gap, then a good acquisition trick is to find something that has a relatively small value to the acquirer, but relatively large value to the target's owners,e.g., the free use of a BMW for a 5 year period!«

Once an agreement has been reached in the negotiations, with respect to the price, the acquirer still has some considerations to make. According to one of the interviewed managers:

»When you have reached a price in the negotiations, then you have to go home and think: »can we defend the acquisition at that price?««

And when the final price has been negotiated, then the deal most commonly has to be approved by the acquiring company's board of directors. One of the interviewed managers made an interesting comment about this approval:

»How large an acquisition our board can accept depends on a psychologically-determined boundary, which varies over time. This boundary depends on our earnings. So improved earnings and profit give more freedom to act and peace from the board.«

The insight of the comment above, i.e., that the board's approval of an acquisition does not exclusively rest on the assessment of the individual investment, was supported by a manager in another case company:

»If you buy a company and it does not turn out to go as well as you thought it would, then you might not get permission by your board to make the next acquisition.«

So, not unexpectedly, previous failures and/or successes with foreign acquisitions are also important because they impart to the acquirer a valuable experience with which to better understand the causes of these successes and failures. Or as was put by a manager with long-time experience with foreign acquisitions:

»You always make mistakes in acquisitions, but they are different each time.«

For this reason, the next subsection will deal with the final phase in the acquisition process, i.e., the integration phase. The section will explore which elements from the integration phase that can be used by both the case study companies and the respondents to the questionnaire in the appraisal of future acquisition targets.

2.3. The Integration Phase: Post Acquisition Initiatives and Results

As mentioned in Chapter 5.2.1, ISS requests its subsidiaries to consider quite early in the acquisition process how they want to integrate a potential target they seek to acquire. They make this request because ISS considers the integration phase one of the most critical steps toward a successful acquisition. Because the integration is planned in advance, the ISS subsidiary making the acquisition is ready, with respect to needed changes in the target company, to start implementation of its plans immediately after the acquisition is effected. In ISS' experience, the speed of integration is most important. Management of the acquiring company, i.e., from ISS' subsidiary, must be present in the acquired company from *day one* to conduct and finish interviews with the acquired company's employees, among other things, as quickly as possible. Any employees to be discharged are informed as quickly as possible. However, because ISS seeks to maintain as low a turnover among cleaning personnel as possible, any possible discharges are usually limited to the management level. It is ISS' experience that full information about these issues creates stability and security among the employees, and as one of the interviewed ISS' managers stated:

»The acquired company's employees will often be in a more desirable working situation after an acquisition since we can provide them with more job security, better materials for cleaning, and so on.«

A solid contract and customer base in a target company are essential for ensuring earning potential[289] in ISS' line of business. Therefore, it is important to secure the

[289] See Chapter 5.2.1.

customer base in the acquired company. It is ISS' experience that this is best done by having the ISS managers visit the customers together with the acquired company's managers and/or previous owners - again as quickly as possible. Besides establishing good contact with the customers, these visits are especially important if the target's name changes after the acquisition. In ISS' case, the ISS name always becomes part of the acquired company's new name because the ISS name imparts a standardized image. In fact, this is part of one of the three elements ISS transfers to the acquired company. These three elements are: the ISS image, the ISS corporate spirit and ISS' knowledge of how to organize work. In summary, both a clear plan and the speed with which the plan is implemented are essential ingredients for securing the success of an acquisition, according to ISS.

The speed with which required changes in the target company are implemented was also mentioned by managers of two of the other case study companies. Both of these companies generally limited their integration with the acquired company. In both companies, the required changes were limited to the controlling and accounting systems, as well as to the seats on the board of the acquired company. A manager of one of the case study companies commented in this respect:

»We run our subsidiaries in a very decentralized manner, and we only want as much information necessary to control our investment.[290] As we only acquirer well-managed companies, we are of the opinion that the management is running their »own« business.«

A similar approach was followed by the other case company:

»We have a *very* strong financial focus on our subsidiaries, but that is about all the help the manager of the subsidiary gets from us: know how about controlling and monetary issues. And money. But not a very tight contact to the our management about the day to day management of the subsidiary.«

In one of the acquisitions made by a case company, the level of integration between the acquirer and the acquired company was very high. In the acquired company, changes were made in production, in marketing strategy and in the R&D department. A new management control system was implemented, and also one of the two top managers was replaced because the previous manager wanted to retire. Making so many changes at a time can be difficult, as the interviewed manager expressed:

»There have been many organizational changes and at the same time we have made quite some investments in the marketing and product resources. But I must say the process of making these changes have been much slower and more difficult than expected. The integration almost always turn out to be much more difficult than you expected.«

The cooperation between the new manager and the top manager who stayed on in the acquired company did not turn out very well. There were several reasons for this, including age differences. The top manager who had stayed on was also a previous

---

[290] That is, the acquired company.

owner of the company, and this played some importance in the difficulties experienced by the acquirer. This manager had become very wealthy after the acquisition and the acquirer felt that he mentally was spending much more time thinking about his money than about running the company. So after mutual agreement, this manager decided to retire, and a new manager was hired. Because new managers were also hired in areas the acquiring company was interested in strengthening, the acquired company basically got a whole new management. The interviewed manager of the acquiring company assessed the effect of this change as follows:

»When you have to change so many top managers in a short time, it is almost impossible to finish any projects while this is going on. It takes both time and money before the new managers are settled down in their new jobs. In return, however, the new management team will not be affected by shadows of the past, and they will be thinking much more alike because they know what the strategy is. The strategy was laid down before they entered the company.«

One of the respondents of the questionnaire had a similar experience:

»It took much longer than anticipated to implement the planned rationalizations in production and administration, among other things, because it turned out to be much more difficult to attract qualified employees.«

The integration phase, as well as the success of the acquisitions, was also addressed in the questionnaire. In this, the respondents were asked to respond to a number of »statements« regarding these and other issues. Table 5.7 shows the respondents' answers.

Table 5.7: »Statements« regarding acquisition process and acquisition's success

Question 2.6: Please respond to the following »statements«. Use the index to indicate how much you agree or disagree with the »statement«.	Index: 1: agree very little; 5: agree very much					Average
	1	2	3	4	5	
	-------number of answers-------					
a. After the acquisitions, we reacted very quickly with respect to dismissals and changes in the operations	2	2	5	6	6	3.5714
b. The acquisition was of strategic importance; thus, the financial analysis was of lesser importance in the decision to acquire	2	3	5	5	6	3.4762
c. Our accounting and controlling systems were implemented very quickly in the acquired company	2	1	3	6	9	3.9048
d. The possibility of obtaining synergies was of great importance to the price we paid for the acquired company	0	4	4	7	6	3.7143
e. We mainly want to acquire well-managed companies	1	2	4	7	7	3.8095
f. It was important to keep the management of the acquired company	2	2	4	9	4	3.5238
g. Green-field investments were not a real alternative to the specific acquisition	0	0	2	3	16	4.6667
h. It was hard to gain access to the internal material we wanted for our appraisal prior to the negotiations	4	9	5	3	0	2.3333
i. The usefulness of the financial analysis turned out to be limited	0	5	8	4	4	3.3333
j. The acquisition was a success as the business strategic goals were reached	3	3	3	6	6	3.4286
k. There were some unforeseen problems with the integration of the acquired company	3	5	8	4	1	2.7619
l The acquired company's economic results are better today than they were at the time of the acquisition*	2	2	5	3	8	3.6500
m. The acquired company's business possibilities have developed more favorably than expected at the time of the acquisition*	3	1	8	7	1	3.1000

* : only 20 respondents answered this question.

The integration of the acquired company was addressed in statements (a), (c) and (f). As is evident from Table 5.7, the findings of the questionnaire support the findings of the multiple case study, i.e., the respondents emphasize quick implementation of their accounting and controlling systems and a fast reaction with respect to dismissals and changes in the target's operations. They also put some emphasis on keeping the acquired company's management after the acquisition. The success of the acquisition was addressed in statements (j) to (m) in Table 5.7, and an overall assessment of the responses to these statements gives the impression that the acquisitions were fairly successful.

As previously mentioned, the integration phase serves as a »test« of both the acquirer's appraisal as well as his acquisition strategy since it is in the integration phase that intentions vis à vis the acquisition have to be carried out. Statements of the acquirer's assessment of his acquisition strategy as well as the appraisal of the target were given in the remaining part of Question 2.6. As is evident from Table 5.7, statements (e) and (g) support the findings of the multiple case study given that the acquirers prefer to acquire well-managed companies and that green-field investments were not a real alternative to the acquisition. Recall that the majority of the case companies had a clear acquisition strategy: they wanted to expand through acquisitions, e.g., to obtain a certain size within a given number of years. This strategically-motivated strategy was also found in the responses to the questionnaire, in which the strategic importance of the acquisition was emphasized in most of the answers to statement (b). The answers also indicated that, in most of the acquisitions, synergies were very important to the price paid for the target company, and that the acquirer generally did not have any problems in gaining access to internal material for the appraisal. Given that the acquisitions made by the respondents of the questionnaire were predominantly friendly acquisitions, as were the acquisitions in the multiple case study, it is not surprising that the acquirer had relatively easy assess to internal material for the appraisal.

3. Summarizing the Findings of the Multiple Case Study and the Questionnaire

It was possible to identify three groups of acquirers by their applied methods of appraisal:

* group 1 consisting of companies using NPV, accounting and strategic models.
* group 2 consisting of companies using accounting and NPV models.
* group 3 consisting of companies using only strategic models.

When these methods were applied in the acquisition appraisal, the application was characterized by:

* a rather short time horizon. Most companies chose six years or less.
* synergies. These were either carefully included or not included at all by the case companies. The possibility of obtaining synergies was of some importance to the respondents in the questionnaire.
* an estimation of synergies/goodwill. This was not determined exclusively by an »objective« assessment, but also by more subjective elements, including »does the estimated price seem to be too high?«, principles etc.

In fact, a number of aspects were generally considered to be important in considering the acquisition of the target company:

* the target had to be a well-managed and preferably profitable company.
* the target should operate within the acquirer's core business area and preferably have a strong market position within its local market.
* the acquisition had to be friendly.

But also, after the targeting, a number of aspects were generally considered important to the appraisal:

* the target's products and growth potential, e.g., with supplements from the acquirer.
* the target's customer base.
* the target's commitments to employees and other parties.
* the appearance of buildings, plants etc.

And an identification was made of a number of problems needing to be overcome in the appraisal:

* it was not always possible *only* to acquire a part of the target company, e.g., a business unit.
* feelings with respect to continuance of the target's name, etc., could be important to the target's owners and thus also to the price.

The studies also identified a number of areas where an appraisal had turned out to be wrong or areas that, according to the acquirer's experience, generally were very important for ensuring the success of an acquisition:

* planned changes often take more time and are more difficult than initially expected.
* a partly new management is not always successful in combination with many organizational changes.
* the integration has to be planned prior to the acquisition, preferably already in the targeting phase, and implemented with speed after the acquisition.
* information about the planned changes should be given to employees and customers in an open manner immediately after the acquisition.

In addition to the aspects mentioned above, the acquirer's experience - either with making acquisitions or with the acquisition country - was generally considered to be important for limiting mistakes in the acquisition appraisal and thus to the success of the acquisition.

CHAPTER 6

A Tentative Theory Applicable to Company Appraisal

The purpose of this chapter is to create a tentative theory applicable for appraising a company. The theory should be able to appraise a company in monetary terms as well as in more strategic terms. The intention is to show that such a theory can be developed by integrating the extended NPV framework[291] with the resource-coherency theory.

Because the theoretical foundation of the extended NPV framework has previously been presented,[292] the first section of this chapter will only present the theoretical foundation of the resource-coherency theory. In the same section, resource-coherency theory will be integrated with the extended NPV framework. The second section of this chapter illustrates how the two integrated theories explain a number of the issues highlighted in the empirical study in Chapter 5. The final section of this chapter summarizes the implications of the tentative theory for acquisition appraisal.

1. The Resource-Coherency Theory: Basic Concepts and Links to the Extended NPV Framework

The concept of resources has been used by several scholars in, more or less, developed theories. However, the resource-coherence theory presented here varies from most of these theories because of the very specific definition of the resource concept. This definition has been elaborated by the Danish philosopher Lennart Nørreklit,[293] and it forms the basis for his resource-coherence theory. [294] In the

---

[291] That is, the NPV principle extended with option theory. See Chapter 4.

[292] See Chapter 4.

[293] L. Nørreklit (1993) and (1995).

[294] L. Nørreklit (1993) and (1995).

following, the resource definition and other fundamental definitions and concepts of the resource-coherence theory will be presented.

According to L. Nørreklit (1996), there are five attributes in the definition of what constitutes a resource for a company:[295]

»A resource to a firm is by definition an entity such that:

1. it is readily *accessible* for the firm
2. it posses certain *potentials* that are realized under certain conditions;
3. it has a *controllable* structure so that controlled acts can activate the resource under the proper conditions;
4. the managers or controllers of the firm posses *methods* to perform controlled acts and thus exert control; and
5. some of its potentials can realize goals or *purposes in the firm's sphere of interest.*«

For an entity to be a resource to a company, all five attributes must be fulfilled. If an entity is not accessible to the company, then evidently it cannot be a resource to it. Similarly, it is not enough that the entity is readily accessible to the company, it must possess the remaining attributes as well to be a resource to the company. Take, for example, the labor market. The »entity« will, in this instance, be »workers«. Even if these workers are readily accessible to the company and all possess certain potentials that can be used to realize purposes in the firm's sphere of interest, i.e., attributes 1, 2 and 5 are fulfilled, they are not resources to the company if they are not controllable and/or if the company does not possess methods for exerting control. The workers will be controllable if they perform the work that the company wants them to perform, and one method for exerting control would be to pay them for their work. Thus, the labor market - or any other market for that matter - does not offer resources to a company, rather it offers input factors which the company has the possibility for turning into resources.

Another important feature of the resource definition is the focus on controllability rather than mere ownership, i.e., a resource need not be owned by the company to which it is a resource. An example of a resource with this feature could be the market to which a company sells its products. Assuming that attributes 1, 2 and 5 are fulfilled, this market would be a resource to the company if the company both is able to control the sale of its products and possesses methods to exert control. Thus, if the company had a long term relationship with its customers and were able to sell its products on a continuing basis to these customers based on this past relationship, then this market would be a resource to the company. In this example, we see how relationships and social control constitutes one way of obtaining and exerting control. Of course, ownership of a factor would also in most cases be a plausible way to obtain control over it - although not always. A management may not be able to make a subsidiary or a group of its employees act according to management's intention. And the owners of the company may have a similar problem in getting

[295] p. 52, author's italics.

management to act the way the owners would like, e.g., to maximize shareholder value. Agency theory is concerned with how owners/management can obtain and exert control over management and employees, respectively. The issue of controllability and the methods for exerting control are also the main focus in network theory, although their recommended method - social control - is rather different from the »reward-punishment« methods recommended by agency theories.

Previously, it has been established that factors are not necessarily resources. Input factors are necessary, but not sufficient for creating a resource. For an input factor to be a resource, it must also possess certain potentials for the company which the company is able to realize through existing methods. We may be able to imagine a world of possibilities in which the input factor may be usable in the company's sphere of interest, but it is only to the extent that we possess methods to realize the potentials embedded in these possibilities that they will become a resource to the company. Thus, by means of a method for exerting control, resources form a bridge between the input factors and their potentials. This issue is elaborated by L.Nørreklit (1995) in the following way:[296]

»A resource is an entity to be found between two abstract extremes: that of pure brute facts and that of pure logical possibility. ....In life world (*sic*) these two extremes are always more or less integrated. ....From *a world of facts* we can by logical reasoning negate the facts and construct *logically possible worlds.* Here facts and logical possible worlds are opposites.. Facts are historical and belong essentially to the past. The logical possible worlds represent the infinite amount of conceivable alternatives *one of which will become the future*....To narrow down the possible alternatives and make the future more controllable, we impose restrictions on the world of possibilities. The restrictions are based on experience and on additional theoretical and factual knowledge of the wold. Thus, we construct the idea of *real possibilities*, i.e. things that de facto can be realized if one has the resources necessary. . . Amongst the universe of real possibilities we may look for those that are our chances or opportunities. *Chances* are something possible within our sphere of interest and not totally out of reach given our resources. *Opportunities* are a little more realistic than chances. An entity is an opportunity if it is within our reach given the resource we have i.e. although it is not directly realizable with the resource we possess, it is supposed that we can achieve the necessary resources by using the resources we do possess. ...Possibilities, chances and opportunities are distinct from *resources.* In these the fact-logic integration is insufficient to guarantee systematic achievement of results. There is no certain method to realize possibilities or opportunities. The outcome of an effort to realize chances or opportunities is uncertain.«

Figure 6.1 shows visually how resources form a bridge between actual facts and future possibilities.

[296] pp. 11-13.

Figure 6.1: Resources between facts and logic, the actual and the possible

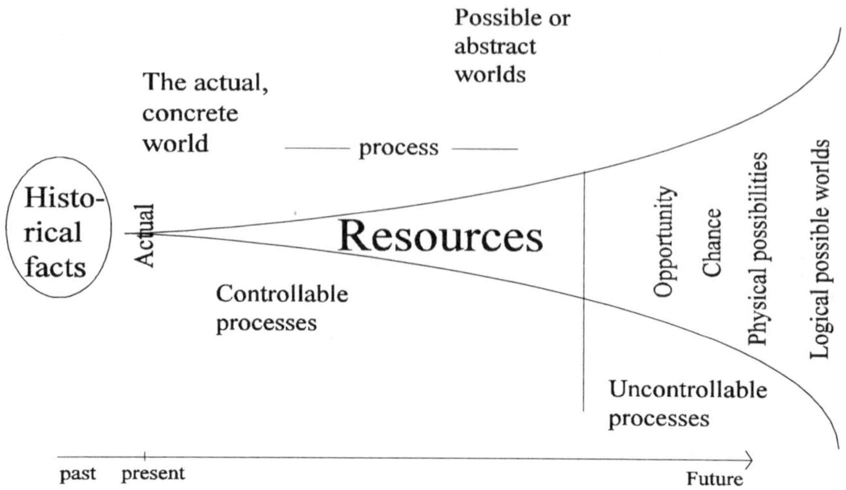

Adapted from L. Nørreklit (1995) with permission.

By examining the presence of the five attributes in the resource definition elucidated above, it is possible to identify the different resources a company possesses and to classify them according to a specific principle, if that is desired.[297] Most resources are possessed by companies for the purpose of performing an activity. To perform an activity, e.g., to produce a product, often several resources will be needed. Furthermore, for the activity to be performed profitably, these resources must *cohere,* i.e., fit together. L. Nørreklit (1995) operates with two types of coherence, as expressed by the following:[298]

---

[297] Such principles could be, for example, business segments, products, departments or purposes. L. Nørreklit (1993), however, classifies resources according to their differences in controllability and the methods which they are applied. For a number of companies, this principle of classification will lead to the identification of the following resources of the company: PRIMARY RESOURCES: 1. social organization of employees, 2. management, 3. strategic/ market resources, 4. financial resources, 5. technology; and SECONDARY RESOURCES: 1. synchronizing resources, i.e., support structures/systems serving to enable an optimal synchronous function of operations, decision making and coordination, 2. diachronizing resources, i.e., resources to support the development and adjustment of the company's other resources. pp. 11-16.

[298] p. 39.

»Resources <u>cohere</u> in quantity and quality. ...Quantitative coherence is a question of efficiency. Efficiency is based on coherence of capacities. If resources do not cohere quantitatively, the firm is unable to utilize some of it's resources, slack will reduce competitive strength of the firm. Qualitative coherence is a question of effectiveness. It concerns the overlap of potentials. If the resource do not cohere in quality, there is insufficient match of potentials. This shows itself in quality problems and consequent deterioration of goal oriented activity. The potentials of the resources cannot be utilized properly.«

Whether the resources of a company cohere depends on the resource profile of the company; this is a structural question. In the resource-coherency theory, it is the coherence of all the company's resources that determines the competitive advantages of the company. To maintain or improve its competitive advantages, a company should try and make it as difficult as possible for other companies to catch up. As is evident from Table 6.1, the characteristics of a resource affect the coherence and thus also the competitive advantages of the company.

Table 6.1: Effects of a resource's characteristics on coherence

Resource Characteristic	Effect on the Coherence
1. The resource is difficult to access/ replicate / substitute a. for the company possessing it b. for the competitors	1.a. Slack is more likely to occur → negative effects on the quantitative coherence 1.b. Negative effects on the competitors' quantitative coherence → negative effects on *their* competitive advantages and positive effects on the competitive advantages of the company possessing it
2. The resource renders several potentials	2. Both qualitative and quantitative coherence are more easily to obtain and improve → positive effects on competitive advantages
3. The resource is easily controlled	3. The resource's potentials are more easily realized → positive effects on the qualitative coherence
4. The methods for exerting control are difficult to replicate/ substitute a. by the company possessing it b. by the competitors	4.a. Qualitative and quantitative coherence are more difficult to obtain and improve → negative effects on competitive advantages 4.b. Negative effects on the competitors' quantitative and quantitative coherence → negative effects on *their* competitive advantages and positive effects on the competitive advantages of the company possessing the resource
5. The resource can be used to realize several purposes	5. Qualitative coherence are more easily obtained and improved → positive effects to the competitive advantages

Note: The above list of characteristics and effects is not exhaustive.

Assuming that the overall aim of company is to generate profit to secure its long term survival, then the company will need to secure input factors, turn these into resources for the purpose of creating an output factor, and sell these at higher prices than were paid for the input factors.[299] This implies that the value of a resource - or a set of resources - will have a lower bound equal to the total value of all its input factors (*input value*) and an upper bound equal to the total value of all its output factors (*output value*). The larger the span between the input and output values, the more profit will be created by the company. The company's resource coherence is determinative by the size of this span. Quantitative coherence is a matter of input/output ratio, i.e., the quantity of input factors used for creating the output factors. Subsequently, an increased quantitative coherence will imply a larger span between the input value and the output value. Qualitative coherence is a matter of output/goal ratio, so an increased qualitative coherence will imply more goals realized in terms of output, i.e., the output value increases, and thus will result in an increased span between input value and output value. In this way, resource coherence can be seen as a leverage between input value and output value.

It is readily seen that the NPV principle can be used within the resource-coherence theory for making various calculations, as is normally done within financial theory. An example would be to calculate whether or not to acquire a set of input factors, given the purpose of creating a resource and a subsequent set of output factors. However, there are parts of a set of resources that cannot be measured adequately by the use of the NPV principle. As previously established, the value of a set of resources has a lower bound equal to the input value and an upper bound equal to the output value. While the input value can be readily measured using the NPV principle, only a part of the output value can be measured by the NPV principle. This becomes evident once a closer look is taken at the output factors generated by the resources and it is realized that these need not consist of unambigious »entities«, but rather they may be compounded. For example, output factors may be compounded of more than mere products; they may also be compounded of, e.g., learning effects, or new opportunities that can be transferred into potentials realizable in the company's sphere of interest and subsequently into new resources,[300] flexibility effects,[301] etc. In fact, some output factors are compounded *solely* of one or several of the latter effects and opportunities.[302] If the output factors

---

[299] Note that a company need not necessarily pay - in monetary terms - for its input factors. See the example of the market as a resource where relationships and social control constitutes the control method.

[300] The output from a R&D process, i.e., diachonizing resources, would be an example of this.

[301] For example, when a company is able to improve its synchronizing resources and obtain a higher degree of resource coherence, e.g., using otherwise slack resources for alternative purposes or by increasing the potentials of the resource. See the section on learning effects.

[302] This may, for example, be true with respect to the output factors from an R&D department.

are set equal to the purposes that a set of resources are to realize, then the output factors can be said to consist of two parts, namely:

1. a part that can be assigned to the realization of *current* purposes in the company's sphere of interest; and
2. a part that can be assigned either to the options of realizing *future* purposes in the company's sphere of interest and/or to the options of realizing these in a more coherent manner.

The part of the output factors falling into the first category would be the services or products that the combined resources of company, division or SBU[303] produces, i.e., the part of the output that, on a current basis, flows from the activity performed with the resource set. This part of the output factors' value - referred to here as *current output value* - can readily be measured in terms of cash flow, i.e., by the use of the NPV principle. This approach, however, is not valid with respect to measuring the part of the output factors falling into the second category because these are the equivalent of the opportunities and flexibility effects of investments. The value of these investments, shown in Chapter 4.3.2, could be adequately captured only by option theory. Thus, both the NPV principle and option theory are needed to measure the value of a resource set adequately.

In Figure 6.2, the determinant of the resource value, and the boundaries that the input value and output value makes on it, are illustrated graphically.

Figure 6.2: Determinants and boundaries of the resource value

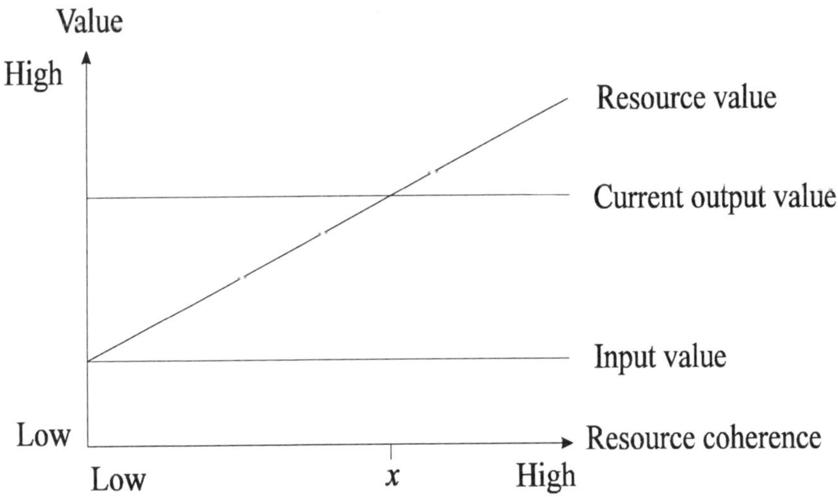

[303] SBU is an abbreviation for strategic business unit.

It is seen from Figure 6.2 that the value of a set of resources (*resource value*) is determined by the resource coherence. The input value forms the lower bound of the resource value. Regardless of the resource coherence, the input value is fixed:[304] it is simply a set of factors bought in their respective markets. The current output value[305] forms the upper bound of the part of the resource value, and it is attributed to the output that, on a current basis, flows from the activity performed with the resource set. This part of the resource value can be measured using the NPV principle. But the current output value also sets a bound on the part of the resource value that can be realized here and now. Thus, even if the resource coherence is higher than indicated by the x in Figure 6.2,[306] the company possessing the resource set cannot currently turn this excess resource coherence into value. However, this does not imply it is unwarranted to try to obtain resource coherence in excess of what can be turned into current output value. On the contrary, this excess resource coherence implies that the resource set possesses opportunities and/or flexibility that can be turned into value in the future. Thus, excess resource value is also a valid part of the total value of a set of resources.

Summarizing, this section has presented the basic concepts of the resource-coherency theory, and it has established the links between the resource-coherency theory and the extended NPV framework. It was shown that, to measure the total value of a resource set, not only was the NPV principle necessary, but so was option theory, i.e., both theories within the extended NPV framework. The establishment of these links shows it is possible to integrate the resource-coherence theory and the extended NPV framework, and thus, provide a tool enabling us to analyze the current state and future potentials of a set of resources - whether they are a company, a division or something else - not only in strategic terms, but also in monetary terms. In this way, each of the analyses provides a check on the other and, used together, they should bring a generally deeper understanding of the strategic choices. This will, hopefully, provide a better analysis that can serve as basis for decisions.

---

[304] The price of an input factor may, of course, vary over time. But in Figure 6.2, we look at the determinants and boundaries of a resource's value at a fixed point in time. Thus, the value of the input factors are assumed to be fixed.

[305] Note that as time is assumed to be fixed in Figure 6.2 (see the previous footnote), the current output value is also assumed to be fixed. Similar to the input value, the output value may vary over time. Furthermore, the output value may also depend on the resource coherence, e.g., the more the output is tailored to its buyers (a matter of resource coherence), the higher a price they may be willing to pay for the output.

[306] Note that x marks the degree of resource coherence that can be turned into current output value, i.e., it marks the x-axis value equivalent to the point of intersection between current output value and resource value.

2. The Resource-Coherency Theory: Explaining the Findings of the Exploratory Study on Acquisition Appraisal

Within the resource-coherence theory, the main difference between a green-field investment and an acquisition is that, in the first instance, factors are obtained, and in the latter instance, resources are obtained. If the input factors are readily available in their respective markets, then green-field investment will be the chosen investment mode if a company only desires to buy input factors. If the input factors are not readily available in a market or if a company wants to buy resources, then acquisitions will be the relevant investment mode.[307] The decision to acquire should, in the context of resource-coherency theory, be taken if and only if the acquirer's analyses show that the acquisition will improve total resource coherence - and thus also total resource value - of the combined companies. In the following, three main categories of means will be identified by which an improved resource coherence can be obtained for the combined companies, i.e., the acquiring and the acquired companies. An improved resource coherence can be obtained:

1. by reducing the amount of slack resources,
2. by transferring methods that can improve resource coherency, and
3. by improving the possibilities for realizing more purposes.

Calling upon the distinctions between quantitative and qualitative coherence, as described in the previous section, it is readily seen that the first category addresses quantitative coherence, the second category addresses both quantitative and qualitative coherence, and the third category addresses qualitative coherence. Dispite acquisition motives may - and often will - be compound, meaning that companies seek to obtain an increased resource coherence by means falling into more than one of the above categories, it has been chosen to adress acquisition motives in connection with each of these categories in the following.

Among the acquisition motives falling into the first category are synergies of scale and scope. In the questionnaire, »the possibility of synergies of scale and scope in production and marketing« was found to be a fairly important acquisition motive for the acquiring company. Also »expectations of increased productivity« and, to a slightly higher degree, »the target's market knowledge« were found to be acquisition motives of some importance. The target's market knowledge may help improve the quantitative coherence of the combined company if there before the acquisition had been a mismatch between production and marketing resources in each of the two companies, e.g., if the acquirer was slack on marketing resources whereas the target company was slack on production resources. However, with respect to the case company that acquired those distributors they felt should be selling more of their

[307] Another possibility would be a joint venture. But due to the focus of this book, this investment mode will be disregarded here.

products,[308] the mismatch was more one-sided in nature. It was the acquirer that had slack resources and who could obtain a higher degree of quantitative coherence by acquiring its distributor. The distributor's quantitative coherence did - at least in principle - not change; its resources were just rearranged so that they served other customers.[309]

The acquisitions this case company made of its distributors are also very interesting from a resource value perspectives for another reason, namely, because they show that a large part of a company's value, i.e., the value of all its collected resources, can consist of »entities« that the company does not own.[310] This will be true if one company chooses to give the control over something it owns to another company.[311] Because the latter was true with respect to this case company and its distributors, the case company was in a favorable position at the time it wanted to acquire the distributor - the distributor's resources would collapse if the case company withdrew the allowance to control the »entity«. Such a withdrawal of the control attribute would leave the distributor with nothing, but a set of input factors - or perhaps some very ill-matched resources. This is a situation that the case company would be able to take advantage of in negotiations. They could argue that payment would only be made for the input value of the distributor's collected resources plus a very small additional amount,[312] in light of the fact the distributor would possess only input factors if the case company withdrew the allowance to distribute its products. In this instance, it is worth noting that the advantage is not only due to ownership of the »entity«, it is also due to the specific attributes of the »entity«, i.e., its difficult accessibility and substitutability.[313] Thus, once again, it becomes evident that, within the resource-coherency framework, it is both the collected attributes of a resource and their interrelationship that creates a resource and determine its value.

The resource-coherence framework implies that slack resources, intended for being brought into better use to improve quantitative coherence, have to be compatible in order for the acquisition to improve, rather than destroy, resource value. The condition of resource compatibility would be expected fulfilled in related

---

[308] See Chapter 5.2.1.

[309] This could, of course, also lead to the deterioration of some resources, e.g., market resources. However, this is disregarded in the following for the purpose of clarity.

[310] A resource need not be owned by a company to which it is a resource. What is important is the control over the resource. See the definition of resources in the previous chapter.

[311] For example, the right to distribute its products.

[312] That is, the intrinsic value of the distributor's company plus a small amount of goodwill.

[313] In Table 6.1 the effects of these resource attributes on resource coherency are shown.

acquisitions,[314] but not in diversifying - or unrelated - acquisitions. This implies, for example, that if an acquirer has slack management resources it wants to transfer in an unrelated acquisition, then the acquirer would actually be transferring only input factors to the acquired company and *not* resources. This is true because the new management would hardly know the acquired company's resources well enough, nor the methods it uses to control these, to be able to realize the purposes of the acquired company that will raise the acquired company's total resource value over it's current level.

Another of the case companies examined, in its acquisition appraisal, whether the target company had slack resources in production by checking if the workers were idle at their machines. Their purpose of doing so was, however, not to combine resources that were slack in the target company and the acquiring company, respectively. Rather it was to transfer their methods to the target company with the purpose of improving the target company's resource coherence. This leads to the third category of means for improving resource coherence, namely the transferral of methods between the acquirer and the acquired company.

One of the managers interviewed in the case study noted that, in his experience, synergies always came in a smaller size, and later, than expected. This implies that, although the compatibility of resources is a necessary condition for improving resource coherence - and thus also resource value, it is not sufficient for doing so. Methods for controlling the resource and for realizing its potentials are also needed.

The above situation characterizes the circumstances surrounding one of the acquisitions made by another case company: the acquisition was within the acquirer's core business, but the methods transferred to the acquired company did not fit with their resources.[315] In this instance, the methods to exert control over the resources transferred from the large acquirer to the smaller acquired company were just too detailed and extensive. Resource coherence was destroyed rather than improved.[316] For yet another case company, however, the difficulties arose in transferring methods from a smaller company to a larger company.[317] From a resource-coherency perspective, it is not the direction in which the methods are transferred, nor the relative size between the transferring and receiving companies, that is important to the success of the transferral. Rather, it is the fit between the resources and the methods for exerting control over the resources that is important.

In the case company ISS, this has been fully realized and they are rather good at transferring methods to the companies they acquire. In all ISS' acquisitions, at least

---

[314] That is, acquisitions where the acquirer and the acquired company have related products, markets and/or technology.

[315] See Chapter 5.2.1.

[316] That is, the acquired company used time for making detailed budgets, strategy plans, etc. that could have been used in a better way.

[317] See the quotation referring to »the golden rule«, p. 103.

two methods are transferred: »ISS' corporate spirit« and »ISS' knowledge of how to organize work«. The purpose of transferring the first method is to maintain the current employees within the company as long as possible: this is of value because, in the cleaning business, the turnover of employees is rather high. The purpose of the latter method is to obtain a higher resource coherency, i.e., to make the employees use their working time more efficiently (quantitative coherence) so that the ISS subsidiary is able to realize more goals (qualitative coherence). ISS has, due to its experience with foreign acquisitions, learned which methods are transferrable between companies and which methods are transferrable between countries.

Within the resource-coherency framework, it is acknowledged that methods have to be learned, and thus, transferring and applying new methods takes time. In their acquisitions, ISS emphasized speed in their transfer and implementation of methods from the acquired company; in their experience, speed was very important to the stabilization, conservation, and subsequently, improvement of the acquired resources.

Other acquirers in the two investigations found that planned changes were often more difficult and more prolonged that anticipated. For reasons similar to those stated above, this is not a surprise from a resource-coherency perspective. Moreover, these planned changes may also imply changes in the mix of resources used to perform an activity. As a result of this, the acquired company's resource coherence will be disturbed for a time until a new state of resource coherency is reached. To the extent the acquirer is not familiar with the acquired company's method attributes[318] and is, therefore, unable to assess the effects of changes in this variable, the acquired company will, for awhile, become more a set of opportunities than a set of resources to the acquirer. Due to the importance of learning effects in the transferral of methods, as elaborated above, the acquirer's experience, with the business segment of the target company, with previous acquisitions, and with the acquisition country's culture, would all contribute to the acquirer's knowledge of the method-attributes likely to be present in the acquired company. This would, subsequently, reduce the time it takes to change the acquired company from a set of opportunities to a set of resources.

ISS recommends that changes be carried out with ultimate speed after an acquisition. If these changes also include changes in the acquired company's resource mix, then resource-coherency theory would also dictate a change in the acquired company's resource coherency. If several changes were to occur over a prolonged period, then the different classes of resources, e.g., management and synchronizing resources, would have to get used to changed attributes, e.g., new methods and purposes, before a new and more stable state of coherence could be obtained.[319] This process would most likely lead to an initial drop in resource

[318] That is, the methods applied to exert control over the resources.

[319] That is, when a change is carried out, the resource set will have a low coherence, which will begin to rise as the learning effects set in.

coherence - and also in resource value - until the new and stable state of coherence were obtained.

The importance of obtaining control of the acquired resources was also represented in the questionnaire by »fast implementation of control systems«, »acquisition of well-managed companies« and »keeping the target's management«. All of these can be seen as elements helping the acquirer to obtain and secure control over the acquired company, and they were all rated fairly high on the scale of importance.[320]

The control attribute is needed to realize the potentials of resources. Quite interestingly, the main focus in the acquirers' appraisal of the target company seemed to concentrate on the target's potentials, the purposes being realized currently, and its opportunities, i.e., the means falling into the category of improving the possibilities of realizing more purposes. This was represented in the questionnaire[321] by »the possibility of faster growth« and the »expectations of increased sale«: acquisition motives that were rated high on the scale of importance. Also »access to an otherwise hard-to-access market« was rated relatively high. The dominant focus in these motives was on an improvement in the acquirers' qualitative coherence, i.e., they focused on improving the goals the acquirer could realize with his current resources.

The focus was the reverse, with respect to some of the acquisitions made by the case companies. In the appraisal of these acquisitions, the target's customer base as well as its growth potentials were assessed. The focus, in combination with the uniqueness i.e. the accessibility and substitutability, of the resources or methods intended to be transferred, determined the acquirer's bargaining power in the negotiations. If the acquirer possessed a resource, or could transfer a method for improving the value of the target company, and the resource/method was fairly unique, then the acquirer would only have to pay a very small amount of goodwill in addition to the market value of the target company. This is because the target company's owners would not be able to increase the value of their company on their own or with another acquirer. If, however, the resource or method were not very unique, then the target company would be in a position to either buy the needed input factors/develop the methods by itself or allow itself to be acquired by another company. Thus, in these instances, the target company would be in a favorable position in the negotiations because it could argue that the acquirer had to pay goodwill in addition to the target company's value. The target company would, namely, be able to improve its value either by itself or by the aid of others fairly easily.

From the above examples, it can be seen how important it is for the competitive position of a company to maintain and improve the attributes of its resources and the resource coherence on a continuing basis. Furthermore, it can be seen that it is the

---

[320] See Table 5.7.

[321] See Table 5.1.

characteristics of resource attributes, their compatibility, and thus, their coherence that creates the competitive advantages of a company.

3. Summarizing the Implications of the Tentative Theory on Acquisition Appraisal

In the two exploratory studies on acquisition appraisal, it was found that most acquirers' generally used more than one method to appraise the target company they sought to acquire. Furthermore, most of these acquirers used either NPV based models in combination with strategic models or exclusively strategic models in their appraisal. Thus this indicates that NPV based models on their own do not provide an adequate foundation for an acquisition decision.

The resource-coherency theory emphasizes the strategic elements of a company, i.e., the resources and their attributes as well as the resources' coherence, and thus enables an acquirer to appraise a potential target from a strategic perspective. The extended NPV framework, on the other hand, focuses solely on transferring these elements into monetary terms. In Chapter 6.1, the links between the resource-coherency theory and the extended NPV framework were illuminated and it was shown that, once these were integrated, it was possible for an acquirer to apply a single approach in acquisition appraisal and to arrive at both a strategic as well as a monetary appraisal. So, in this respect, acquirers' requirements, for a foundation upon which decisions can be made, are met.

Within the resource-coherency theory, the decision to acquire is taken if and only if the acquisition will improve total resource coherency - and thus total resource value - of the combined companies.

Slack and compatible resources in the acquiring and acquired companies are indicators of a possibility for improving the collected quantitative coherence of the combined companies. Similarly, new potentials or possibilities, expected to appear as the result of an acquisition, are indicators of possibilities for improving the collected qualitative coherence of the combined companies. But even if these indicators - or other indicators - are necessary conditions for improving quantitative and qualitative coherence, respectively, they are not sufficient: methods for realizing these possibilities are also needed. Thus, resource-coherency theory puts emphasis on the method attribute of an resource. Within the literature on acquisition strategy, methods have not generally been an emphasized feature. But as is evident from the findings of the two exploratory studies, the realization, in particular, of the potentials of an acquisition, often turn out to be more problematic than anticipated by the acquirers' i.e., the acquirers do not seem to possess the necessary methods to realize the potentials. Thus, emphasis on methods seems warranted.

When changes are made in the mix of a set of resources, then its coherence will also change. The immediate effect of this will be for resource coherency to drop. After awhile, resource coherency will increase as resources become more suited to realize their intended purposes. When resources are able to do this fully, then a new and stable state of resource coherency will be obtained. Once this new and stable state of resource coherency has been reached for the combined companies after an acquisition, resource coherency should be higher than before the acquisition. This is a condition for the acquisition to be successful within the resource-coherency framework.

The value of a resource is determined by the resources attributes and their interrelationship. With respect to the value of a set of resources, resource coherency also needs to be considered. A distinct feature of the resource-coherency framework is that »entities« need not be owned, but only controlled for them to be a resource to a company. This implies that a company may be able to generate output value - and perhaps also resource value in excess of the output value - from »entities« it does not own. However, as was exemplified in the previous chapter, the ownership of an »entity« becomes important in more extreme situations, e.g., acquisitions, because the resource value could deteriorate, leaving the company, to which the »entity« was a resource, with nothing more that its remaining input factors.

With respect to the price paid for »entities« owned by the company for which they are resources, the price would be larger than the resources' current output value in an acquisition situation. The extent to which the price paid for the resource would exceed the current output value depends on the bargaining power of the acquiring and the target companies, respectively. Their bargaining power would be determined by the direction and uniqueness, i.e., accessibility and substitutability, of the resources or methods to be transferred between these two companies.

Concluding, it can be said that, above all, the resource-coherency framework stresses the importance to a company to maintain and improve both resource attributes and the resource coherency of it's resources on a continuing basis if it wants to stay competitive. The resource-coherency framework points out that the resource attributes and the resource coherency also determine the value of resources and thus the value of the company.

CHAPTER 7

Implications of the Book

1. Main Results of the Book

In this book, the financial appraisal of acquisitions has been addressed from two perspectives: a stock market perspective and an acquiring company perspective, respectively.

The aim of the book has been, within each perspective, to account for the theories on acquisition appraisal and to test these theories empirically to the extent possible. As the meta-theoretical assumptions of this book are based in critical rationalism, as elaborated by Popper, Popper's schema of the scientific process has been used in addressing this aim. With respect to the stock market perspective, presented in Part 1, it includes the two elements of Popper's schema of the scientific process, namely, »theory« and »error-elimination«.[322] With respect to the acquiring company perspective, presented in Part 2, it includes three elements, namely, »error-elimination«, »problem« and »theory«.

In Part 1, the »theory» element was elaborated using Lakatos' methodology of scientific research programmes (MSRP) as an explanatory framework. This means that the theories on acquisition appraisal from a stock market perspective were not presented by themselves, but rather in connection with the hard core assumptions and the negative and positive heuristics of the MSRP to which they belong. In addition to the criticism of the theories, the »error-elimination« element was addressed mainly by empirically testing the assertions deduced from the theories to the extent this was possible with the available data. The major finding of these tests can briefly be recapitulated as follows:

[322] I.e. $T_1 \rightarrow D_1 \rightarrow E_1$ in the schema presented in the text on page 16 which are equivalent to »TT → EE« in Popper's original schema cf. note 32.

* The Danish stock market reacts more quickly with respect to acquisition announcements coming from »major acquirers« than from »other acquirers«.
* The $CAR_{[t=-5;5]}$ is statistically significant and positive for »other acquirers« as well as for »all acquirers«.
* The $CAR_{[t=-5;5]}$ is statistically significant and negative for »major acquirers«.
* The $\overline{AR}_t$ is statistically significant and positive on event day t = 0 for »foundation-owned acquirers«, but statistically insignificant on event day t = 1 and on all event days for the other ownership types.
* The acquirer's ownership structure was not important to shareholder value as none of the *DAR*'s, with respect to different types of ownership, were statistically significant.
* The hard core's hypothesis of an unbiased price reaction was supported, with respect to the Danish stock market's reaction to a sample of Danish international acquisitions made during the period 1988-1992, when compared with the assessment of acquisition made by managers of the acquiring companies.

In Part 2, Lakatos' MSRP was also used as an explanatory framework with respect to the theories on financial appraisal of acquisitions from an acquiring company perspective. However, in this part of the book, the purpose in elaborating the net present value (NPV) research programme was to address the »error-elimination« element. Since the theories in this research programme all are logical theories, error-elimination focused on which investments the theories could be applied to and on the recommendations scholars could make to operationalize these theories. The findings of »error-elimination« were an important part of the input to the »problem« element, as they illuminated theoretical aspects of the problem of how acquisition appraisal on a company level could be improved. As the »problem« also has an empirical side, this was illuminated by means of two empirical studies exploring Danish companies actual appraisal of their own international acquisitions. Finally, a tentative theory was suggested as a solution to the »problem«. This tentative theory combines the resource-coherency theory with the extended NPV framework by developing a set of assumptions about the value of resources. The relevance of the tentative »theory« as a solution to the »problem« is shown by applying the tentative theory to the findings of the two exploratory studies.

2. Implications for the Stock Market Perspective on Acquisition Appraisal

Among scholars, and thus also in the literature, the stock market perspective on the financial appraisal of acquisitions has by far been the most dominant of the two perspectives. Within the stock market perspective, research interest has concentrated on testing whether acquisitions create shareholder value or not. Based on the findings of empirical studies, a number of more or less developed theories have been advanced. In this book, two of the most complete theories in this area - Roll's »hubris hypothesis« and Jensen's »free cash flow hypothesis« - have been elaborated and criticized. A number of less developed theories or assertions have also been discussed. With respect to the choice of these theories, the book is conventional.

However, the presentation of these in the context of Lakatos' MSRP as an explanatory framework is not. By using Lakatos' MSRP as an explanatory framework, this book contributes by making the implicit assumptions of these theories, i.e., the hard core of the research programme to which they belong, explicit.

The test methodology used, i.e,. the event study, is also conventional as it is the most commonly used test method within this area of research. However, this book differs from the main stream of empirical studies within this area with respect to its choice of data, i.e., *international* acquisitions, as by far the dominant choice of data has been national - and predominantly U.S. - acquisitions. The findings in the empirical studies on *domestic* acquisitions have generally been that, on average, acquisitions do not appear to create shareholder value, whereas the limited number of studies on *international* acquisitions have found the opposite to be true, namely that, on average, shareholder value was created.[323] The findings of this book confirm the findings of the studies on international acquisitions. The findings here found that, for the total sample, i.e., »all acquirers«, shareholder value in a 11-day event window was positive and statistically significant. None of the theories within this area try to explain the empirical finding that international acquisitions in contrast with domestic acquisitions, on average, create shareholder value.[324] Thus, further theoretical development is warranted in this respect.

The book also addressed the issue of whether acquisition frequency, i.e., how often an acquirer makes acquisitions, was important to shareholder value. To the author's knowledge, this issue has not been addressed before in the literature. The semi-strong form of the market efficiency hypothesis asserts that security prices reflects all publically-available information. This implies that acquisition announcements by acquirers having a stated acquisition strategy[325] and making international acquisitions on a frequent basis do not contain much new information to the market. Thus, if the sample were to be divided into two subsamples, with one subsample, »major acquirers«, representing those companies making acquisitions on a frequent basis and the other subsample, »other acquirers«, representing the remaining companies making acquisitions on a rare basis, then it would be expected that the stock market's reaction would be *stronger* with respect to announcements from »other acquirers« than from »major acquirers« due to the greater amount of new information. The market efficiency hypothesis does not lead us to conclude that the *direction* of the stock market's reactions should differ with respect to the two samples. However, Roll's argument - in his »hubris hypothesis« - that the lack of

[323] See e.g. Markides & Ittner (1994) and Doukas & Travlos (1988).

[324] For reasons of completeness it should be noted that some studies e.g. Harris & Ravescraft (1991) have examined whether a number of variables - including tax and industry variables - were able to explain value gains in acquisitions. However, these variables were not a part of a well specified theory.

[325] I.e. which have explicitly mentioned acquisitions as a strategy in their annual reports.

recurring acquisitions in the managers' careers is the reason why they do not account properly for the winner's curse, would lead us to assume that the stock market's reaction - if measured exclusively in terms of the direction - would be most favorable with respect to the subsample »major acquirers«.

The findings of this book supported the assertions above with respect to *size* but not *direction* of the stock market's reaction. The Danish stock market's reaction was statistically significant and positive for the subsample »other acquirers« and statistically significant and negative for the subsample »major acquirers«. Thus, the findings support the market efficiency hypothesis and they do not support Roll's »hubris hypothesis«. The findings are rather paradoxical as the stock market in this manner seems to »punish« acquisition experience. As no theories apparently give a plausible explanation for this empirical finding, further research on these issues is warranted. This research would, first and foremost, examine whether this paradox is found in other data, and second, if so, develop a plausible explanation - or a tentative theory - of the paradox.

Since the ownership structure of listed Danish companies is unique in that a large proportion of companies are foundation-owned or family-owned in contrast to diversified ownership predominating in many countries, the book also tested whether the acquirers' ownership structure was importan to the shareholder value created in their acquisitions. The tests performed did not, however, find any statistically significant differences in the shareholder value created with respect to subsamples representing different types of ownership.

The final series of tests performed in Part 1 had the purpose of examining whether the assumption, in the hard core of the market efficiency research programme, of an unbiased price reaction was supported with respect to the applied data. Using the assessments made by managers of the acquiring companies of their own acquisitions as a measure of the actual acquisition result, it was not possible to reject the unbiasedness hypothesis. Thus, the hard core of the market efficiency research programme has once again been supported in this book.

This latter support of an unbiased price reaction also implies that the findings on the stock market level are applicable to the company level - that is, with respect to an average assessment of the acquisitions. But what are the implications of this with respect to the appraisals of target companies made by acquiring companies? Well, if their acquisition announcements generally are followed by positive price reactions in the stock market, then we would expect the actual acquisition results to turn out positively; the opposite would be expected of negative price reactions in the stock market. However, this does not in any way help the companies for whom the actual acquisition results are expected to be negative. They still need help on how to improve their acquisition appraisal.

3. Implications for the Acquiring Company Perspective on Acquisition Appraisal

The issue of how acquisition appraisal on a company level is improved was addressed in Part 2 of the book. In the financial literature, this issue has not received much attention, neither theoretically nor empirically. Theoretically acquisition appraisal has been viewed as just another investment decision to which the existing theories readily can be applied. The book illuminates these existing theories by using Lakatos' MSRP as an explanatory framework. In doing so, it was pointed out that the NPV principle, which constitutes the hard core of the NPV research programme, faced some problems: the problem of applying the NPV principle to some types of investments, the problem of misapplication of the NPV principle by practitioners, and the lack of empirical predictions in the NPV research programme because all the theories belonging to it are logical theories. The book emphasized that the problem of applying the NPV principle to some types of investments had been solved theoretically by extending the NPV principle with option theory, but that the latter two problems, which were of a more empirical nature, still remained to be solved.

Although this book's elaboration and assessment of the NPV research programme could be viewed as a part of »error-elimination« in Popper's schema of the scientific process, it can also serve as the theoretical part of the input to the »problem« element of Popper's schema. The empirical part of the »problem« was addressed in the book by conducting two exploratory studies - a multiple case study and a questionnaire, respectively - on how Danish acquirers had actually appraised their international acquisitions. The findings of these two exploratory studies included that:

* Strategic models were widely used in acquisition appraisal and that NPV models were never used alone.
* The possibility of obtaining synergies, i.e., project interactions, as well as the target's growth potentials, i.e., growth options, were both important in acquisition appraisal.
* It was not always possible to acquire only the part of the target company that the acquirer wanted.
* The integration phase was very important and it was often more difficult and prolonged than expected.

These findings did not in themselves lead to a solution, i.e., »tentative theory«, for the »problem«. Rather they served as inspiration for »inventing«[326] it. The tentative theory that this book has put forward as a solution to the »problem« combined the resource-coherency theory with the extended NPV framework by developing a set of assumptions of the value of resources. It was shown that resource-coherency theory enabled the acquirer to appraise a potential target from a strategic perspective, whereas the extended NPV framework enabled him to appraise the target in

---

[326] According to Popper there does not exists any logical method for coming up with a new theory; the best we can do is simply guess! See also Popper (1959), p. 458 (appendix: a translated letter from A. Einstein): "...and I think (like you, by the way) that theory cannot be fabricated out of the results of observation, but that it can only be *invented*." Authors italics.

monetary terms. Thus, both the scholars' and the practitioners' requirements for the foundation of an investment decision were met in the tentative theory.

The tentative theory also put forward a number of assertions with respect to acquisition appraisal including:

* The decision to acquire should be taken if and only if the acquisition is expected to improve the total resource coherency - and thus the total resource value - of the combined companies.
* Slack and compatible resources in the acquiring and acquired companies, respectively, are indicators of possibilities for improving the combined companies' quantitative coherency.
* New potentials or possibilities, expected to appear as the result of an acquisition, are indicators of possibilities for improving the combined companies' qualitative coherency.
* While the above mentioned indicators are necessary conditions for improving the quantitative and qualitative coherency, respectively, they are not sufficient. Methods for realizing these possibilities are also needed.

There are several theoretical as well as empirical implications of the tentative theory. First, since the basic concepts of the tentative theory[327] are logical in nature, this implies that it is not possible to falsify these concepts empirically. However, with respect to the tentative theory's applicability to acquisition appraisal - or any other investment decisions for that matter, it is possible to test the tentative theory's operationality as well as the validity of its statements. Although the book has addressed both issues[328] by applying the tentative theory to the findings of the two exploratory studies, a significant amount of research is still needed, including the elaboration on the statements of the tentative theory. With respect to acquisition appraisal, this would encompass an elaboration on which categories of resources are compatible and thus indicators of quantitative and qualitative coherency, as well as an elaboration on which - and to which extent - methods are transferrable across borders. Several authors have offered insight on these issues in related areas,[329] and it may be possible to incorporate these insights into the tentative theory. Nonetheless, a significant amount of work - empirically as well as theoretically - still remains in this area. Similarly, the operationality of the tentative theory needs to be examined. This issue should be addressed empirically, and in this respect, qualitative research methods, e.g., case studies, need to be employed.

Moreover, it could be interesting to examine if the tentative theory were also applicable to the market level and to which extent. For example, with respect to the stock market's reaction to acquisition announcements, the following argument could be put forward within the tentative theory:

---

[327] I.e. the definitions of resources, resource coherency, resource value etc as well as the NPV principle and growth options.

[328] Note: it was not an aim of this book to test the tentative theory - it was solely put forward as a solution to the »problem» identified with respect to the existing theories on the financial appraisal of acquisitions.

[329] See e.g. Kogut (1985) and Collis & Montgomery (1995)

»Recall that the stock market does not deal with resources - it deals with factors.[330] When a company bids on a target listed on the stock market, then the target's stock price will rise. This is, however, not an indication of the factor being turned into a resource, as the target's owners still not are able to exert control over the target company. Rather it is an indication of the factor being a limited input factor the bidding company. Because the resource value of this limited factor to the bidder is higher than the input value, then the target's owners will be in a position to exploit this and gain in the stock price in excess of the factor price. Thus, if the bid is dropped, then we would expect to se a drop in the target's stock price - in principle, back to its old level - as the factor, i.e., the stock, no longer would be a limited factor to the bidder nor would the owners of the target company be able to control it and thus gain its resource value.«

But also in this area, a significant amount of empirical as well as theoretical work still remains.

As it stands though, the tentative theory does provide practitioners with a feasible tool for a monetary as well as a strategic acquisition appraisal on a company level.

4. Concluding Remarks

This book has addressed the financial appraisal of acquisitions from two perspectives: a stock market perspective and an acquiring company perspective. As the two previous sections of this chapter indicate, a great amount of research is still needed within each of the perspectives.

However, I had a purpose in presenting *two* perspectives on the financial appraisal of acquisitions rather than elaborating one perspectives in even greater detail. This purpose was to show that there are two sides to acquisitions and acquisition appraisal: to show that both managers of acquiring companies and their stockholders are appraising acquisitions and that there are differences in how each of the parties conducts this appraisal, and to show the implications of the appraisals for the theories within each of the respective areas.

I find that a number of managers regard acquisitions as »their« business and look at the stock market reaction's to an acquisition announcement with some surprise, and perhaps also some indignation. But they should know that acquisitions are not solely their concern; acquisitions are also the concern of their stockholders. On the other hand, I understand why managers sometimes look upon the stock market's reaction to their acquisition announcement with astonishment. Especially when the stock market reacts with negative price changes to acquisitions carried out by experienced acquirers in which the acquirers are able to realize synergies and thus create real value.

The theories on the financial appraisal of acquisitions as they stand are not currently able to comprehend both perspectives on acquisition appraisal. The book has pointed out that the development of a theory comprehending both perspectives

---

330 The stock market only deals with resources to the extend that the shares are sold in such large quantities that the buyer is able to control the company in which he buys stocks and also possess the methods to exert this control.

would be fruitful mainly because it would guide acquirers toward those acquisitions worth carrying out and which to avoid, without limiting them from making the value-creating acquisitions the stock market perspective currently views as »bad« investments. Furthermore, such a theory would also increase our understanding of the pricing mechanism on the stock market and thus be applicable to areas other than acquisition appraisal.

The book has suggested that the tentative theory presented in Chapter 6 might be a plausible path toward the development of a theory comprehending both perspectives. There is obviously a great deal to be done, however, before this tentative theory can be converted into a more complete theory comprehending both perspectives. Hopefully, this book has contributed to this eventuality by drawing attention to the subject, inspiring other researchers' interests in this area, so they may want to contribute to the work yet to be done.

Appendix A

Table A1: $\overline{AR}_t$ *and* t_t*-values, on event days and samples. Estimation period: 60 days before and 60 days after the event window*

Event day, t	Major Acquirers (N = 27)			Other Acquirers (N = 15)			All Acquirers (N = 42)		
	$\overline{AR}_t$ in %	t-value	positive : negative	$\overline{AR}_t$ in %	t-value	positive : negative	$\overline{AR}_t$ in %	t-value	positive : negative
-5	-0.51	-2.12*	14:13	0.09	0.24	8:7	-0.30	-1.46	22:20
-4	-0.13	-0.56	12:15	0.15	0.41	10:5°	-0.03	-0.16	22:20
-3	0.36	1.50°	14:13	0.51	1.37°	8:7	0.41	2.03	22:20
-2	-0.25	-1.04	8:19*	-0.04	-0.10	8:7	-0,17	-0.86	16:26°°
-1	0.27	1.14	18:9°°	-0.11	-0.29	5:10°	0.14	0.67	23:19
0	-0.28	-1.16	9:18°°	0.01	0.03	5:10°	-0.18	-0.86	14:28**
1	-0.23	-0.96	9:18°°	0.41	1.11	7:8	-0.00	-0.01	16:26°°
2	0.10	0.40	12:15	0.58	1.57°	9:6	0.27	1.32	21:21
3	0.24	1.01	19:8*	-0.09	-0.25	6:9	0.12	0.60	25:17°
4	-0.12	-0.51	11:16	0.76	2.05°°	12:3**	0.19	0.95	23:19
5	-0.33	-1.38	11:16	0.09	0.26	7:8	-0.18	-0.88	18:24

°, °°, *, **: The null hypothesis, $\overline{AR}_t$ equal to zero, is rejected at a 90%, 95%, 97% or 99% - or better - level of confidence (one tailed test).

Appendix B

Growth option value and the project's NPV as functions of the project's gross present value

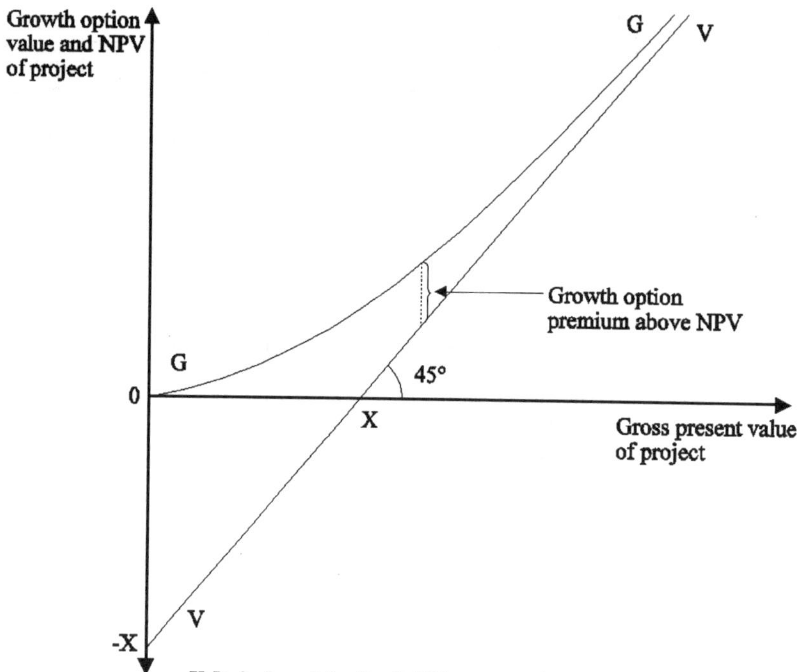

X: Project's capital outlay; VV: Net present value op project corresponding to various asset values; GG: Growth option value corresponding to various asset values.

The GG-curve will collide with the 0XV-curve as time approaches the final exercise date. At the exercise date the two curves will be identical. The difference between the growth option value and the NPV of the project is referred to as the option's time value, within the framework of traditional option theory.

Appendix C

A simple option valuation formula
Source: Kester (1993) p. 205

$$(10)\quad G_t = \frac{G^+_{t+1} * (1 + r_f - R^-_{t+1}) + G^-_{t+1} * (R^+_{t+1} - 1 - r_f)}{(1 + r_f) * (R^+_{t+1} - R^-_{t+1})}$$

where

G_t	=	value of growth option in the current period
G^+_{t-1}	=	value of growth option in the next period, assuming that the underlying asset have risen in value
G^-_{t-1}	=	value of growth option in the next period, assuming that the underlying asset have fallen in value
R^+_{t-1}	=	factor by which value of underlying assets will rise under favorable conditions (e.g., a 20% increase in the value would be represented as 1.2)
R^-_{t-1}	=	factor by which value of underlying assets will fall under unfavorable conditions (e.g., a 20% decline in the value would be represented as 0.8)
r_f	=	risk-free, one-period rate of return expressed as a fraction.

For a project with only one period before expiration, G^+_{t-1} and G_{t-1} are the project's NPV, one period hence, under favorable and unfavorable conditions, respectively. In states of the world in which NPV is negative and the value zero used for G_{t-1} in the above formula.

For projects with several years before expiration, the above formula can be applied recursively to arrive at a growth option value in the present. An example of this is given on the next page.

Appendix C (continued)

Assumptions

Capital Outlay (million $)	PV of Expected Cash Inflow (million $)	Gain in PV from a Prior Success (%)	Loss in PV from a Prior Failure (%)
70	65	20	20

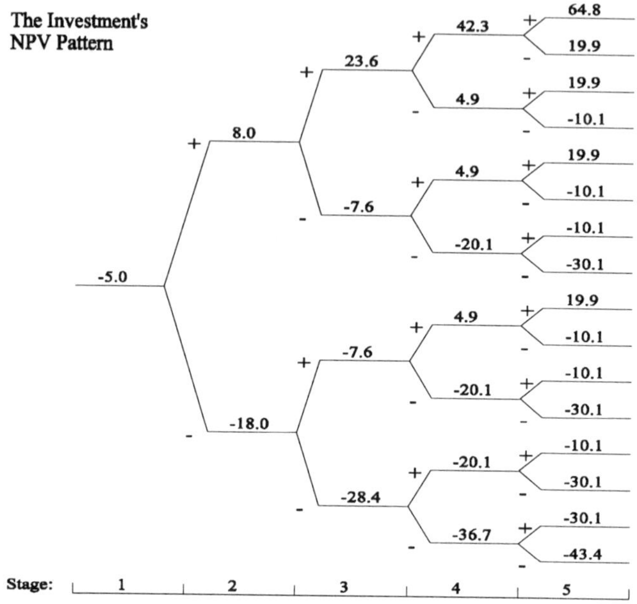

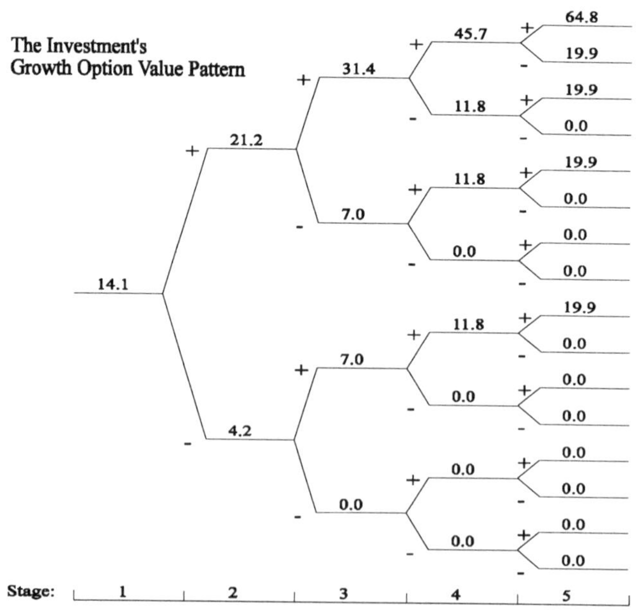

Selected Bibliography

The literature addressing the issues dealt with in this book is vast, and it includes both the strategic and the financial literature on acquisitions, acquisition appraisal, and international and national investment decisions. The author owes a great deal to this literature as it has nourished my interest of the topic and also, in a more indirect manner, influenced the book and its structure. In the following, I have, however, chosen only to present a list of the literature which has influenced the book in a more direct manner and has been used directly or has directly affected the book.

Aharoni, Y.: *The Foreign Investment Decision Process.* Harvard University Press, 1966.

Arbnor, I. & B. Bjerke: *Företagsekonomisk metodlära.* Studentlitteratur. 1977.

Ackenhusen, M.: *ISS - International Service Systems A/S.* INSEAD, 1993.

Bradley, M., A. Desai & E.H. Kim: "Synergistic Gains From Corporate Acquisitions and Their Division Between the Stockholders of Target and Acquiring Firms." *Journal of Financial Economics,* May 1988, pp. 3-40

Brealy, R.A. & S.C. Myers: *Principles of Corporate Finance.* McGraw-Hill, 1988.

Brown, S.J & J.B. Warner: "Measuring Security Price Performance." *Journal of Financial Economics*, 1980, vol. 8, pp. 205-258.

Brown, S.J & J.B. Warner: "Using Daily Stock Returns - The Case of Event Studies." *Journal of Financial Economics,* 1985, vol. 14, pp. 3-31.

Collis, D.J. & C.A. Montgomery: "Competing on Resources: Strategy in the 1990s." *Harvard Business Review*, 1995, July-August, pp. 118-128.

Conn, R.L.: "A Re-Examination of Merger Studies that use the Capital Asset Pricing Model Methodology." *Cambridge Journal of Economics,* 1985, vol. 9, pp. 43-56.

Conn, R.L. & Connell, F.: "International Mergers: Returns to U.S. and British Firms." *Journal of Business Finance and Accounting*, 1990, vol. 17, no. 5, pp. 689-711.

Danmarks Statistik: *Statistical Yearbook*, various years.

Dixit, A.K. & R.S. Pindyck: *Investment under Uncertainty.* Princeton University Press. 1994.

Donaldson, G.: *Managing Corporate Wealth.* Praeger, 1984.

Doukas, J. & N.G. Travlos: "The Effect of Corporate Multinationalism on Shareholders' Wealth: Evidence from International Acquisitions." *Journal of Finance*, 1988, vol. XLIII, no.5, pp. 1161-1175.

Eiteman D.K., A.I. Stonehill & M.H. Moffet: *Multinational Business Finance.* 6th ed. Addison-Wesley Publishing Company, 1989.

Elling, J.O. & M. Christiansen: *Strategisk regnskabsanalyse og virksomhedsvurdering.* FSRs Forlag, 1993.

Elton, E. & M. Gruber: "Efficient Markets." In: *Modern Portfolio Theory and Investment Analysis.* 1991.

Estrup, C.: "Internationslisering af dansk erhvervsliv via virksomhedopkøb." *Ledelse & Erhvervsøkonomi,* no. 4, 1988.

Estrup, C.: *Udlandets overtagelser af virksomheder i Danmark.* Handelshøjskolens Forlag. 1989.

Fama, E.F: "Efficient Capital Markets: A Review of Theory and Empirical Work." *Journal of Finance*, vol. XXV, no. 2, 1970, pp. 383-417.

Fama, E.F: *Efficient Capital Markets: II.* Journal of Finance, vol. XLVI, no. 5, 1991, pp. 1575-1617.

Greens 92, vol. 1 & 2.

Gregory, A.: *Valuing Companies: Analyzing Business Worth.* Woodhead-Faulkner, 1992.

Harris, R.S. & D. Ravenscraft: "The Role of Acquisitions in Foreign Direct Investment: Evidence from the U.S. Stock Market." *Journal of Finance,* 1991, vol. XLVI, no. 3, pp.825-844.

Hunt, J.W.: "Changing Patterns of Acquisition Behaviour in Takeovers and the Consequences for Acquisition Processes." *Strategic Management Journal*, 1990, vol. 11, pp. 69-77.

Hunt, J.W., S. Lee, J.J. Grumbar & P.D. Vivian: *Acquisitions - the Human Factor.* Egon Zehnder International, 1987.

Hymer, S.H.: "The Large Multinational 'Corporation': An Analysis of Some Motives for the International Integration of Business." An English Translation from: *Revue Economique,* vol. 19, no. 6, 1968, pp. 949-73.

Jarrell, G.A. & A.B. Poulsen: "The Returns to Acquiring Firms in Tender Offers: Evidence from Three Decades." *Financial Management*, Autumn, 1989, pp.12-19.

Jarrell, G.A., J.A. Brickley & J.M. Netter: "The Market for Corporate Control: The Empirical Evidence Since 1980." *Journal of Economic Perspectives*, 1988, vol. 2, no. 1, pp. 49-68.

Jensen, M.C.: "Some Anomalous Evidence Regarding Market Efficiency." *Journal of Financial Economics*, vol. 6, 1978, pp. 95-101.

Jensen, M.C.: "Takeovers: Folklore and Science." *Harvard Business Review,* 1984, November-December, pp. 109-121.

Jensen, M.C.: "Agency Costs of Free Cash Flow, Corporate Finance, and Takeovers." *American Economic Review*, vol. 76, no. 2, 1986a, pp. 323-329.

Jensen, M.C.: "The Takeover Controversy: Analysis and Evidence." *Midland Corporate Finance Journal*, Summer, 1986b, pp. 6-32.

Jensen, M.C.: "Takeovers: Their Causes and Consequences." *Journal of Economic Perspectives,* 1988, vol. 2, no. 1, pp. 21-48.

Jensen, M.C. & W.H. Meckling: "Theory of the Firm: Managerial Behavior, Agency Costs and Ownership Structure." *Journal of Financial Economics*, vol. 3, 1976, pp. 305-360.

Jensen, M.C. & R.S. Ruback: "The Market for Corporate Control." *Journal of Financial Economics*, 1983, vol. 11, pp. 5-50.

Johanson, J. & J.E. Vahlne: "The Internationalization Process of the Firm A Model of Knowledge Development and Increasing Foreign Market Commitment." *Journal of International Businsess Studies,* 1977, vol. 8, pp.23-32.

Kester, W.C.:"Turning Growth Options Into Real Assets." In: Raj Aggarwal (ed.): *Capital Budgeting Under Uncertainty*. Prentice Hall, 1993.

Knudsen, C.: *Økonomisk metodologi. Om videnskabsidealer, forklaringstyper og forskningstraditioner*. Jurist- og Økonomforbundets Forlag. 1991.

Kogut, B.: "Designing Global Strategies: Comparative and Competitive Value-Added Chains." *Sloan Management Review*, Summer 1985, pp. 15-28.

Kogut, B.:"Designing Global Strategies: Profiting from Operational Flexibility." *Sloan Management Review*, Fall 1985, pp. 27-38.

Kogut, B.: "Country Capabilities and the Permeability of Borders." *Strategic Management Journal,* vol. 12, 1991, pp. 33-47.

Kogut, B.: "Joint Ventures and the Option to Expand and Acquire." *Management Science*, vol. 37, no. 1, 1991, pp. 19-33.

Kogut, B. & N. Kulatilaka: "Options Thinking and Platform Investments: Investing in Opportunity." *California Management Review,* 1994, Winter, pp. 52-71.

Kogut, B. & H. Singh: "The Effect of National Culture on the Choice of Entry Mode." *Journal of International Business Studies,* 1988, Fall 1988.

Kogut, B. & U. Zander: "Knowledge of the Firm, Combinative Capabilities, and the Replication of Technology." *Organization Science*, 1992, vol. 3, no.3, pp. 383-397.

Kogut, B. & U. Zander: "Knowledge of the Firm and the Evolutionary Theory of the Multinational Corporation." *Journal of International Business Studies*, 1993, Fourth Quarter, pp. 625-645.

KonkurrenceRådet: *Fusioner og virksomhedsovertagelser 1992*. 1993.

Lang, L.H.P., R.M. Stulz & R.A. Walkling: "Managerial Performance, Tobin's Q, and the Gains from Successful Tender Offers." *Journal of Financial Economics,* vol. 24, 1989, pp. 137-154.

Lai, V.S. & Trigeorgis, L.: "The Strategic Capital Budgeting Process: A Review of Theories and Practice." In: Trigeorgis, L.(ed.): *Real Options in Capital Investment.* Preager, 1995.

Lakatos, I.: *Beviser og gendrivelser*. Århus Universitet. 1989.

Lakatos, I.: "Falsification and the Methodology of Scientific Research Programmes." In: Lakatos & Musgrave (eds.): *Criticism and the Growth of Knowledge*. Cambridge University Press. 1970.

Lakatos, I.: *Philosophical Papers.* Volume 1. Edited by J. Worrall and G. Currie. Cambridge University Press. 1978.

Lubatkin, M. & R.E. Shrieves: "Towards Reconcilaiation of Market Performance Measures to Strategic Management Research." *Academy of Management Review,* 1986, vol. 11, no. 3, pp. 497-512.

Lønroth, H.L. & D.M. Reeb: *Market Efficiency: The Case of Denmark.* Unpublished Working Paper, Aarhus School of Business, 1994.

Madsen, O.Ø.: *Virksomhedsovertagelser og fusioner i dansk industri.* Nyt Nordisk Forlag Arnold Busck. 1983.

Magee, B.: *Karl Popper.* Nyt Nordisk Forlag Arnold Busck. 1973.

Markides, C.C. & C.D. Ittner:"Shareholder Benefits from Corporate International Diversification: Evidence from U.S. International Acquisitions." *Journal of International Business Studies,* 1994, 2nd quarter, pp. 343-366.

Montgomery, C.A. & V. A. Wilson: "Research Note and Communication: Mergers that Last: a Predictable Pattern?" *Strategic Management Journal*, vol. 7, 1986, pp. 91-96.

Morck, R., A. Shleifer & R.W. Vishny: "Do Managerial Objectives Drive Bad Acquisitions?" *Journal of Finance,* Vol. 45, no. 1, 1990, pp. 31-48.

Mukherjee, T.K. & G.V. Henderson: "The Capital Budgeting Process: Theory and Practice." *Interfaces*, vol. 17, no.2, 1987, pp. 78-90.

Myers, S.C.: "Finance Theory and Financial Strategy." *Interfaces,* vol. 14, no.1, 1984, pp. 126-137.

Nørreklit, H.: *Virksomhedens problemerkendelse.* Jurist- og Økonomforbundets Forlag. 1991.

Nørreklit, H.: *Økonomistyring i praksis - hvordan man virkeliggør teorierne.* WP: G nr. 3. Aarhus School of Business. 1993.

Nørreklit, L: *Resources and the Firm.* Working Paper, Aalborg University, 1993.

Nørreklit, L: *Resource-Coherency Theory of the Firm - A Relativity Theory of the Firm.* Working Paper, Aalborg University, 1995.

Nørreklit, L: "A Resource Construction of the Firm" In: Nørreklit, L. & H.M. Schoenfeld (eds.): *Resources of the Firm; Creation, controlling and accounting.* Jurist- og Økonomforbundets Forlag. 1996.

Pedersen, F.: Nutidsværdimetoden til kreditvurdering. *Finans/invest*, no. 2, 1994, pp. 19-23.

Pedersen, T., P. Schultz and H. Vestergaard: *Danske virksomheders etableringer i udlandet.* Handelshøjskolens Forlag. 1993.

Popper, K.R.: *The Logic of Scientific Discovery.* Hutchinson & Co Ltd. First published in 1959, 10 ed. (revised) 1980.

Popper, K.R.: *Conjectures and Refutations.* Routledge & Kegan Paul plc. First published in 1963, 5 ed. (revised) 1989.

Popper, K.R.: *Objective Knowledge.* Oxford University Press. First published in 1972, revised ed. 1979.

Popper, K.R.: *Kritisk Rationalisme.* Nyt Nordisk Forlag Arnold Busck. 1973.

Roll, R.: "The Hubris Hypothesis of Corporate Takeovers." *Journal of Business,* vol. 59, no. 2, 1986, pp.197-216.

Schultz, P., J. Strandskov and H. Vestergaard: *Hvor internationale er danske virksomheder?* Managements Erhvervspolitiske Forum. 1986.

Segelod, E.: *Capital Investment Appraisal: Towards a contingency theory.* Student-litteratur. 1991.

Servaes, H.: "Tobin's q and the Gains from Takeovers." *Journal of Finance*, vol. LXVI, no. 1, 1991, pp. 409-419.

Smith, G.: *Investments.* Scott, Foresman & Company. 1990.

Stonehill, A. & K. Dullum: "Corporate Wealth maximization, Takeovers, and The Market for Corporate Control." *Nationaløkonomisk Tidskrift,* 1990, no. 1, pp. 79-96.

Strandskov, J.: *Studier i danske virksomheders internationaliseringsprocesser.* Dr.merc. dissertation. Department of International Business, Aarhus School of Business, 1994.

Strandskov, J., S. Thomsen & T. Pedersen: *Ejerforhold og konkurrenceevne i dansk erhvervsliv*. Erhvervfremme Styrelsen, 1994.

Sørensen, B.G.: "Regnskabsinformation og aktiemarkedets effektivitet." *National-økononomisk Tidskrift*, 1982, no.2, pp.224-241,

Thaler, R.H.: "Anomalies: The Winner's Curse." *Journal of Economic Perspectives*, vol. 2, no. 1, 1988, pp.191-202.

Trautwein, F.: "Merger Motives and Merger Prescriptions." *Strategic Management Journal*, vol. 11, 1990, pp. 283-295.

Trigeorgis, L.: "Real Options: an Overview." In: Trigeorgis, L.(ed.): *Real Options in Capital Investment.* Preager, 1995.

Trigeorgis, L. & S.P. Mason: "Valuing Managerial Flexibility." *Midland Corporate Finance Journal*, Spring, 1987, pp. 14-21.

Ugebrevet Mandag Morgen: "Erhvervsledere giver børsanalytikerne topkarakter." No. 29, August 29th, 1994, pp. 17-21.

van Vught, F.A.: "Pitfalls of Forecasting." *Futures*, April 1987, pp. 184-196.

Weaver, S.C., R.S. Harris, D.W. Bielinski & K.F. MacKenzie: "Merger and Acquisition Valuation." *Financial Management,* Summer, 1991, pp. 85-96.

Weston, J.F., K. S. Chung & S.E. Hoag: *Mergers, Restructuring and Corporate Control.* Prentice-Hall International Editions, 1990.

Yin, R.K.: *Case Study Research - Design and Methods.* Sage Publications. 1994.